To my friend

DR. G. NORMAN VICK

Research Oceanographer

*Whose theory of African ballast rock
and our trips to the wreck of the* Empire Mica
provided the idea for this book

Sinkings, Salvages, AND Shipwrecks

ROBERT F. BURGESS

AN AUTHORS GUILD BACKINPRINT.COM EDITION

Sinkings, Salvages, AND Shipwrecks

Sinkings, Salvages and Shipwrecks

All Rights Reserved © 1970, 2000 by Robert F. Burgess

AN AUTHORS GUILD BACKINPRINT.COM EDITION

Published by iUniverse.com, Inc.

For information address:
iUniverse.com, Inc.
5220 S 16th, Ste. 200
Lincoln, NE 68512
www.iuniverse.com

Originally published by American Heritage Press

ISBN: 0-595-00632-9

Printed in the United States of America

PICTURE CREDITS

American Numismatic Society, 67. Atlantic Mutual Insurance Company, 132. Bibliothèque Nationale, 24. Trustees of the British Museum, 119. Black Star, Endpapers. Brown Brothers, 156, 162, 162-3, 163, 164-5, 169, 170-1. Culver, 24, 168. Exquemelin, *Bucaniers of America* (1684), 96. Collection of Mrs. William Tudor Gardiner, Boston, 110. Greek National Museum, 27. *Harper's Pictorial History of the Civil War* (March, 1862), 50. *Harper's Weekly* (1863), 57. *Harper's Weekly* (1888), 148. Herrara's *Decades* (1726), 71. *The History and Lives of Most Notorious Pirates*, 101. Collection of Oliver Jensen, 54-5. Collection of Wilmarth Lewis, 122. Library of Congress, 44, 51, 53. Collection of Alfred Mayor, 4-5. National Maritime Museum, Greenwich, England, 66-7, 98. New York Historical Society, 51. New York Public Library, 119. New York Public Library Map Room, 62-3. New York Public Library, Arents Collection, 144-5. New York Public Library, Rare Books Division, 66, 136, 143. *New York Times*, May 8, 1915, 169. J. Mack Moore Photographic Collection, Old Court House Museum, Vicksburg, Mississippi 154. Kenneth M. Newman, Old Print Shop, New York, 58. Old Dartmouth Historical Society Whaling Museum, New Bedford, Massachusetts, 133. The Peabody Museum, Salem, Massachusetts, 132. *Pirate's Own Book* (1837), 88. The Real Eight Company, 72, 78, 79. Swedish Information Service, 8, 13, 14, 14-5, 15, 16, 17, 18, 19, 20. Underwood and Underwood, 162. UPI, 32. Wide World, 174, 176, 186-7.

Contents ❧❧❧

One of these carved wooden lion's heads decorated each gunport on the seventeenth-century Vasa.

CHAPTER ONE

The Archaeology of Shipwrecks

*I*t was a gay, festive crowd that gathered on the quay before the royal palace in Stockholm on an August Sunday in 1628. The people were there to celebrate the maiden voyage of the largest, most splendid warship in the Swedish fleet. The *Vasa*, named for the royal family, was a showpiece of Swedish boatbuilding. When she left port, she would carry with her the hopes and prayers of a nation already locked in what historians would call the Thirty Years' War.

A cheer arose as sails unfurled and swelled like billowing clouds from the *Vasa*'s towering masts. A murmur of awe swept the spectators as the great galleon swung slowly away from her berth. The figurehead on her bow—a gilded lion with bared claws and fangs—glittered in the afternoon sun. Along her trim oaken hull two tiers of cannon waited to answer a German emperor's threat to invade Scandinavia. Over the sixty-four gleaming bronze muzzles were sixty-four raised gunports, each carved with a golden lion's head against a blood-red background.

Gradually the galleon gathered speed on a gentle southwesterly breeze and whispered across the rippled blue harbor toward the open sea. Then, less than a mile from shore, a sudden gust of wind heeled the *Vasa* sharply to port. Instead of righting herself, she settled lower in the water. The crew began to haul her heavy cannon to starboard to correct the dangerous list, but by then it was too late. Water was already pouring in through the open lower gunports. Before the startled eyes of the spectators on the quay, the great warship settled on her beam-ends and sank like a stone in 110 feet of water. Of more than four hundred people aboard, fifty lost their lives. The day that had begun in triumph ended in tragedy.

Thirty years later salvagers, using primitive diving bells, managed to fish up fifty-three of the ship's sixty-four bronze cannon, but after that even her exact location was forgotten.

The warship lay undisturbed for 326 years until a Swedish Admiralty engineer named Anders Franzén became interested in her. As a boy, Franzén had been enthralled by his father's stories of old shipwrecks along the Swedish coasts. He read everything he could find on the subject, and for many summers he dragged grapnel hooks along the bottom, fishing up fragments of old wrecks. He had often been puzzled to find that old ships' timbers he had located along Sweden's south and east coasts were never riddled by the woodboring teredo worms that had attacked wrecks along the west coast. (Later he learned that shipworms thrived only in water with a high degree of salinity, and that Baltic water was too sweet for them.)

Franzén reasoned that any wooden wrecks he found along the Baltic coasts should be fairly well preserved. He began compiling a list of these shipwrecks, and among them was the *Vasa*.

"Find the *Vasa*," a famous Swedish historian told him, "and you will find the richest treasure of all."

From that moment on, Franzén focused all his efforts on locating the long-forgotten galleon. He spent years studying old maritime records, ships' logs, military archives, and ancient charts. By 1956 he had amassed a staggering amount of information, including a valuable clue from a letter written the year that the ship sank. It mentioned that the *Vasa* had gone down less than three hundred yards from the Island of

Beckholmen. Franzén already had a contour map of that area and he had noticed that the echo-sounding equipment traced a prominent hump on the harbor bottom just south of the Beckholmen dry dock. Engineers had told him that it was probably rock debris from the dry dock, but now Franzén wondered.

Armed with a core sampler of his own design—a six-pound pointed steel cylinder resembling an aerial bomb attached to a strong line—he motored out over the hump and dropped the instrument overboard in 110 feet of water. When he reeled it up, he found in the sharp, hollow nose of the sampler a piece of black, close-grained oak.

Franzén knew that only the finest sixteenth- and seventeenth-century ships were made of this wood, and that in those waters oak would not turn black unless it had been submerged for at least one hundred years. But what if he had sampled nothing more than an old log?

Franzén took cores at several sites over the hump and each time came up with another plug of waterlogged oak. Did he dare hope that he had at last found the *Vasa*?

The Swedish Royal Navy came to Franzén's assistance with a diving vessel and a veteran helmet-and-hose diver named Per Edvin Fäulting.

While Fäulting descended into the gloomy waters off Beckholmen, Franzén waited anxiously at the telephone linking him with the diver. The first reports were not encouraging. Fäulting had landed in a sea of silt; visibility was very poor.

"I'm standing up to my chest in porridge," he told Franzén over the telephone. "Can't see a thing. Should I come up?"

Franzén agreed that he might as well.

Seconds later Fäulting said, "Wait a minute. I just put out my hand and touched something hard. It's wood . . . a wall of wood! It's a ship, all right . . . a big one! I'm climbing up the hull now . . . there are square openings here . . . they must be gunports." Seconds later he said, "Here's another row of gunports. . . ."

There was only one local wreck with double tiers of gunports. Franzén had found the *Vasa*!

What followed was an accomplishment unique in the annals of salvaging: the raising and restoration of a wooden vessel the size and age of the *Vasa*.

Financed by the Swedish government, industry, and private subscribers, the ambitious project got under way in 1958. The *Vasa* measured 210 feet long including her 30-foot bowsprit. Helmeted Swedish Navy divers risked their lives to dig six tunnels beneath the ballasted wreck. Then steel cables six inches in circumference were passed under the hull and attached to two huge pontoons on the surface. A Stockholm salvage firm carefully eased the wreck out of the mud and shifted it onto a firmer bottom in fifty feet of water. Divers then boarded up all gunports and made the vessel reasonably watertight. Inflatable pontoons were attached to the hull, powerful pumps began emptying her of water, and finally, after three hundred years, the galleon was refloated and towed into dry dock at Beckholmen.

Amid the tons of mud that were flushed from the ship's interior, archaeologists found twelve complete human skeletons. Gundecks that were customarily painted red so that guncrews were less likely to be affected by the sight of blood on them bore few traces of the original paint, but all the planking was solid. Early salvagers had smashed through the ship's upper deck to grapple for cannons below, and all the superstructure—the masts, cabins, and a portion of the high-pitched stern—had long ago been obliterated by anchors dropped from vessels overhead. But what remained of the galleon was in astonishingly good condition. To prevent the waterlogged wood from drying too rapidly and deteriorating, sheets of plastic were tied over the top. The entire vessel had to be hosed down regularly until it could be treated with polyethylene glycol, a wood preservative that drives out moisture and strengthens the fibers. Among the many artifacts recovered from the wreck site were bronze cannon, carpenter's tools, wood sculptures, pewter tankards, clay pipes, a leather slipper, and the huge carved lion that had snarled defiance from the prow of the ancient galleon.

Salvaging the ship took six years and cost $2 million, but it ranks as one of the biggest, most successful efforts in salvage history. The *Vasa* is the oldest fully documented ship preserved in the world today.

To appreciate fully how fortunate the salvagers were, one must understand what usually happens to a ship once it slips beneath the surface of the sea. As it sinks, it will either nose dive or plane toward the bottom. At the moment of impact, cargo may shift, seams may open, and parts

TEXT CONTINUED ON PAGE 21

This elaborately carved crowned lion was found aboard the Swedish warship Vasa.

With a displacement of 1,400 tons (compared to the May-
flower's 400 tons), the Vasa was the largest ship in the
Swedish navy when she was built in 1628. A cutaway view
of the floating fortress (left) reveals her many decks. Below,
in a seventeenth-century rendition, is Stockholm, where the
Vasa was built for service in the Thirty Years' War. She
had not even cleared the harbor on her maiden voyage when
she sank in 110 feet of water by the Island of Beckholmen.
Three decades later the majority of her sixty-four bronze
cannon were salvaged with the help of primitive diving bells
like the one at the right. When these bells were lowered to
the bottom, pressure forced the water to the divers' necks.

15

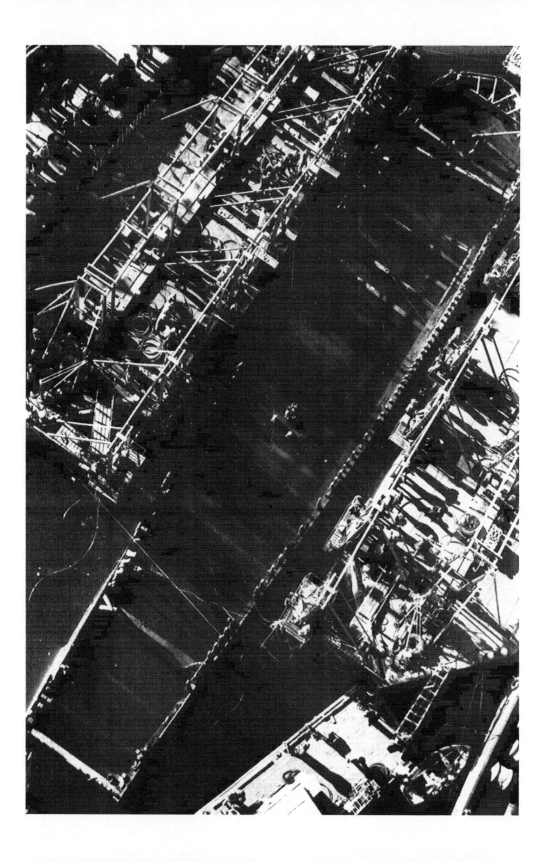

More than three hundred years after she went down, the Vasa broke the surface of the Baltic flanked by two submersible pontoons named the Oden and the Frigg (opposite). To raise her, divers made six tunnels under the warship and passed twelve heavy steel cables through them. The cables were secured to the pontoons, which were filled with water until their decks were awash. Then, very slowly, the pontoons were pumped out until the taut cables eased the warship free of the bottom (right). Above is one of twelve well-preserved human skeletons found aboard the ship — the surviving remains of the fifty men who perished in the course of the disaster.

5M.

32M.

A substantial number of artifacts were discovered in and around the Vasa during the salvage operation. Many of them were very well preserved by the comparatively sweet waters of the Baltic. Among the finds were the carved head opposite and the pewter tankard at left. Below, salvagers winch up one of the sixty-four cannon that were to have made the Vasa such a redoubtable foe.

The Vasa is shored up in dry dock before a permanent structure is built around her. At the right is a view of the lower gundeck as it has been restored. It was flooded when a gust of wind heeled the ship to port, submerging the open gunports.

of the vessel may break away. If the ship lands on rocks or reefs in tropical seas where marine plant and animal life are most active, its rapid destruction is practically assured. If it lands on sand or mud in these waters, its eventual burial will slow, but not stop, deterioration. If, however, the vessel is covered with protective mud in cold, relatively fresh waters such as those of the Baltic, where shipworms and other destructive organisms are virtually nonexistent, then the wreck stands a good chance of surviving intact for centuries. This was the case with the *Vasa.*

Exposed timbers are slowly honeycombed by shipworms, while any metal on the wreck is undergoing deterioration of another kind. When iron, brass, copper, zinc, and a variety of other metals are immersed in salt water, the combination creates in effect a gigantic galvanic battery. Disintegration occurs by the process of electrolysis, in which a current of electrons is set up between two metals of different molecular weights in the presence of an electrolytic solution (salt water). Iron, for example, gradually changes to iron oxide (rust). The first apparent effect of this process is an accumulation of a crust of sand or limy deposit over all metallic surfaces. As the corrosion continues, the object becomes encased in limestone. This white limy layer provides an ideal base for countless larval sponges and coral animals, which in turn build layers of limestone at the rate of one half to two inches a year. Certain forms such as the stinging coral, *Millepora,* cover some surfaces like coats of yellow, orange, and brown paint. Within this shell, metals continue to break down until only a powder remains. In a matter of years, what was once a recognizable ship is hardly distinguishable from the rest of the irregular coral reef bottom.

It is nature's camouflage that makes the discovery of ancient wrecks so difficult for marine archaeologists. Moreover, the contents of the cargo may not necessarily remain with the wreck. As Mendel Peterson, Chairman of the Department of Armed Forces History at the Smithsonian Institution, says in his book *History Under the Sea:* "The ship may strike a reef, ride over it severely damaging its bottom, sail on for several hundred yards, and then go down in a spot far removed from the place where it first hit. In striking it may have lost overboard some of its rigging and guns. In many cases, guns and other heavy objects are jettisoned by the crew to lighten ship after it first struck. After the ship was thus lightened it became more buoyant and sailed on, gradually sinking and finally going down far inside the reef. If the bottom of the ship had been badly opened in striking, it could have spilled out cargo as it sailed to its doom, scattering a path of objects behind it. After sinking, if in an open sand bottom, the hulk would be moved about by current and wave action as it rotted away. It is possible for a hulk to move hundreds of yards over an open sand bottom as the cumulative result of severe storms. At the very least the ship will turn on its side or roll about as it disintegrates, dumping its contents into the sand beside it and thrashing about that which may remain in the timbers. In this manner the ship's contents are jumbled and scrambled so that objects are frequently . . . found far from their original location in the ship. . . .

"Another variation encountered in thick reef areas is that in which the ship strikes a reef tossing equipment and cargo on top of the reef or into a sand hole and then floats on to sink in another. This is a type especially prevalent in the Bermuda reefs, where there are tremendous reef flats with moderately shallow water interspersed with deep holes having sand bottoms. . . ."

As a third possibility, a ship may strike and then sink between reefs in a comparatively restricted area. Under these circumstances it will usually come to rest in an upright position and be protected from wave action by the reefs. The hull will move up and down until it disintegrates. If it is a sand bottom, the cargo will usually be found under the ship's hull, resting against the keel.

When a wreck is covered by coral, archaeologists look for piles of ballast rocks—the stones carried in the holds of old ships to give them weight and balance. These smooth stones were usually round or egg-shaped and no more than a foot in diameter. When a vessel was ripped open by a jagged reef, the ballast usually tumbled out first. Since large sailing ships carried tons of ballast, heaps of smooth rocks on the ocean floor often point like an arrow toward the final resting place of the wreck.

The next things to look for are unnaturally straight lines, or any man-made forms or shapes on the bottom. The distinct shape of cannon protruding from the coral or lying exposed on the bottom is another indication of a fertile site. Early vessels traveled heavily armed with these easily identifiable guns, many of which bear breech marks that often readily establish the nationality and date of the wreck.

Once archaeologists feel they have located a wreck site, they take great pains to see that nothing is disturbed until they are prepared to excavate it methodically. Small underwater buoys are placed to mark prominent points. Underwater metal detectors are used to locate concentrations of buried metal, and these "hot spots" are also buoyed. The site is then laid off on a modified grid.

There are several ways of laying a grid. Sometimes a strong metal rod topped with a revolving ring is driven into the bottom at the center of the area to be excavated. This is called a datum point and it is the mark from which all measurements are made and all grid lines run. First, measurements and compass bearings are taken from this point to all the metal "hot spots." Then, the grid's two base lines are staked out. They intersect each other at right angles at the datum point. Other lines are run at six- to ten-foot intervals from and parallel to the base line, and stakes are placed at each point of intersection, until the entire site is covered.

The site is then mapped or photographed from above so that the exact location of any visible remains can be easily plotted in relation to the grid. Only now does systematic excavation begin, square by square until the entire grid has been searched to a depth of about a foot. The process is then repeated in foot-deep layers, to any desired depth. The precise location of every find is noted on the gridded map so that archaeologists can later reconstruct an accurate record of what happened at the wreck site.

Excavation is done with airlifts, water jets, and hand tools. An airlift is an open-ended metal tube, one end of which hovers just above the ocean floor while the other end leads into a barge on the surface. Compressed air is blown up the pipe from the bottom and the resulting suction vacuums up sand, mud, and small objects and deposits them, usually in a sieve, in the barge. Water jets are high-pressure hoses with a special nozzle that feeds some of the water backward to counteract the jet action of the stream, which would otherwise make the hose difficult to manage. Water jets are mainly used to move soft sediment quickly. Their disadvantage is that they merely shift material without

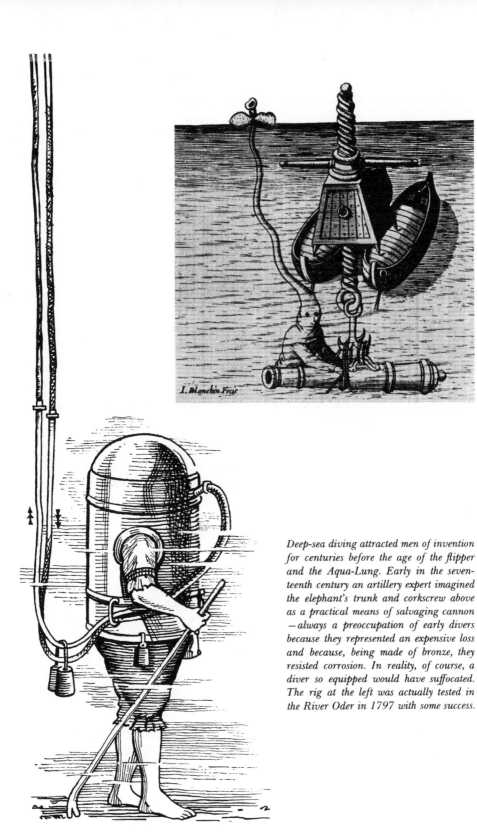

L. Blanchin Fecit

Deep-sea diving attracted men of invention for centuries before the age of the flipper and the Aqua-Lung. Early in the seventeenth century an artillery expert imagined the elephant's trunk and corkscrew above as a practical means of salvaging cannon — always a preoccupation of early divers because they represented an expensive loss and because, being made of bronze, they resisted corrosion. In reality, of course, a diver so equipped would have suffocated. The rig at the left was actually tested in the River Oder in 1797 with some success.

removing it as an airlift does. Hand tools may range anywhere from a weighted ping-pong paddle to a pneumatic drill operated by compressed air from above. The paddle is used by a diver to fan away small amounts of sand as he works slowly through "pay dirt" — a stratum of bottom rich in artifacts.

Underwater archaeology had its beginning seventy years ago, but only since the invention of the Aqua-Lung in 1943 has the science captured the imagination of scores of divers. It is far easier to teach archaeologists to dive than it is to teach divers archaeology. Still, it is often the diving enthusiast rather than the underwater archaeologist who chances upon the unusual find. Such was the case in Antikýthēra, Greece, in the summer of 1900.

A crew of Greek sponge divers were on their way home from a successful trip along the North African coast when a gale forced them to take shelter at the small uninhabited island of Antikýthēra, almost within sight of the Greek mainland. The captain suggested that they look for sponges while they waited out the storm. Diver Elias Stadiatis was helped into his helmet suit and climbed over the side. When he reached bottom, 150 feet down, he was startled to see around him on the sea floor huge images of men, women, and animals. Some were of white marble; others were of dark bronze. Many were partially buried so that legs and arms thrust grotesquely out of the mud as if reaching for the astonished diver.

Stadiatis knew that no one would believe him unless he returned to the boat with some evidence. Reaching down, he grasped a blackened hand and tugged a bronze arm out of the mud.

After examining the find, Captain Demetrios Kondos immediately donned his diving suit and went down to see it for himself and to make careful measurements of the site.

When the sponge boat reached its home port of Symē, Captain Kondos called a meeting of the village elders to discuss what should be done. It was apparent that his divers had found a number of valuable ancient Greek statues, but they were at a depth far below sponge divers' usual working range. To salvage the hoard they would risk death or permanent injury from the bends.

The rest of the summer was spent planning the project with archaeologists from the National Museum in Athens. It was late November before the actual salvaging got under way, and from the beginning there were problems. Hardly had the divers begun work when a severe storm forced them to stop while the ships took shelter. On the first dive, however, they recovered two large marble statues, a life-size bronze head, and a number of smaller pieces. In the weeks that followed, the weather continued bad, and in the rough seas the ships were in continual danger of being smashed against the rocky cliffs. The first statues had come up easily enough, but the rest had to be dug out of the mud — an exhausting task for the six divers working to the limit of their endurance in 150 to 170 feet of water. Their primitive equipment allowed them to remain at these depths for only five minutes before surfacing. If they stayed longer, they would run the risk of a nitrogen build-up in their blood, which would result in the bends. The statues were covered with slime and constantly slipped from rope slings as they were being winched up to the surface. Those that fell back into the ooze frequently crushed others beneath them. Even on days when the weather was good, one hour's work on the bottom was the most that could be accomplished.

After nine months only three of the original six divers were still working. Two of the others were permanently crippled, and one man had died from the bends. Four replacement divers were brought in, and work continued.

The results of those courageous Greek sponge divers' efforts today fill an entire gallery at the National Museum in Athens. Nearly thirty magnificent life-size figures of horses and men stand in the courtyard. The finest of the bronzes is the "Athlete," a fourth-century B.C. work that is larger than life size and none the worse for its long immersion in the sea. Unfortunately, the marble statues did not fare as well. Those parts of the statues that were buried in the mud are in good condition, but the areas exposed to salt water are pitted and eroded by marine organisms, so that the statues appear to have been disfigured by some horrible disease.

Beneath the statues, buried in mud and sand, the divers found the remains of a Roman merchant ship. Various artifacts, including the delicate mechanism of a unique astronomical clock, enabled Greek archaeologists to date the wreck to the first century before Christ. Apparently the ship had been carrying the statues back to Rome as spoils of

The fourth-century B.C. bronze "Athlete," right, and the head of a philosopher, below, were among nearly thirty Greek sculptures found quite by accident in 1900 off the island of Antikýthēra, near Crete. The find was made by Greek sponge divers blown off course while returning from North Africa. The fruits of their long and hazardous salvage operation are now in the National Museum at Athens.

war when disaster—a storm perhaps—sent the overloaded vessel to the bottom. Whatever the cause of the wreck, the eventual recovery of the valuable cargo by a team of divers directed by archaeologists inaugurated the era of underwater archaeology.

In 1948 the French scuba-diving pioneer Henri Broussard, swimming along the bottom of the Mediterranean near Cannes, pulled a graceful earthenware vessel from under a clump of weeds. It was an amphora, used by the Greeks and Romans to store wine or olive oil. Broussard explored further, finding hundreds of the jars strewn haphazardly around an area that contained evidence of at least three shipwrecks. The outline of one ship was clearly visible. Some of the amphorae were the kind used during the first century B.C. During an excavation of the site one of the amphorae was found to have its stopper still in place. An inscription on the stopper was written in the Oscan alphabet, an early language spoken by one of the original tribes of central Italy long after Latin became the official language of Rome. The French scientist Jacques Heurgon translated the inscription and found that it contained the names "Marcus" and "Caius Lassius." After a long search Heurgon finally found the family name among the inscriptions on tombs at Pompeii in southern Italy. Further research revealed that the Lassius family were wealthy wine merchants, which accounted for their names on the amphora's stopper. Its presence on a Roman cargo vessel off the coast of France indicated that the ancient firm of Marcus and Caius Lassius had consigned a shipment of their wine to some Mediterranean port; but it never arrived. One wonders if they ever learned what happened to it. Certainly they could never have guessed that their names would be remembered because of an inscription on an amphora of their wine that had lain undamaged on the bottom of the sea for over two thousand years.

In 1958 an underwater photographer and archaeological assistant, Peter Throckmorton, began a two-year odyssey that led to the oldest shipwreck ever found. In the port of Bodrum, Turkey, he learned that a sponge-diving captain from Istanbul had found some "rotten bronze things" in an old wreck off Cape Gelidonya, on the south coast of Turkey, near Finike. The bronze was so badly corroded that the Turkish divers had received a poor price for the salvaged metal. Throckmorton had never heard of bronze so decayed that it could be called rotten, and he wondered whether it could have come from an ancient wreck of the Bronze Age. When the divers described flat ingots of bronze shaped like animal hides and equipped with leglike handles; a spear point, a knife, and a sword of bronze, Throckmorton felt certain that he was on the right track. He noted the wreck's location and returned a year later equipped to investigate the site. For days the divers searched the rugged reefs off Cape Gelidonya without success. Just as they were about to give up, one of them discovered hunks of coral-encrusted bronze on the bottom. Under the limy deposits were spear points unlike anything the men had ever seen before.

"There's a lot more of them down there," the diver exclaimed, "and a bunch of big flat pieces of metal shaped like oxhides!"

The wreck lay on a bed of sand encircled by large boulders. Dozens of ingots were cemented together so firmly by encrustations that a crowbar was needed to pry them apart. Under the ingots, in a depression in the sand, were crude pottery, bronze spear points, and ax heads. Wooden fragments of the wreck had been preserved by copper salts released during corrosion of the bronze ingots, which were believed to be items of barter with a value equal to that of a cow or an ox. Archaeologists at the University of Pennsylvania and at Princeton University dated the artifacts as typical of those used in Cyprus in the fifteenth and fourteenth centuries B.C. Throckmorton had found a ship that had sunk more than three thousand years ago.

The next year he returned with a full-scale archaeological team that recovered more than a ton of bronze and copper artifacts, pottery shards, scarabs from Syria inscribed with hieroglyphics, scales and weights, tools, weapons, and a fragment of basket made of rope and matting. It will take archaeologists years to analyze the find for a more complete picture of how Bronze Age man lived.

Coins and cannon are the basic pieces of evidence that usually enable archaeologists to establish the age and nationality of a shipwreck, for both frequently bear the date that they were cast and other identification marks. Bits of pottery are also useful in dating because ancient pottery styles frequently changed as often and as radically as modern clothing styles. Finally, for greater accuracy, there is the carbon-14 dating method. All substances that can be reduced to carbon contain the radioactive isotope carbon-14. By knowing the isotope's "half-life" — the length of time it takes atoms of the sample to disintegrate into nitrogen (5,700 years) — it is not difficult to calculate the approximate age of a specimen simply by measuring how much of the isotope is left. The process is accurate to within plus-or-minus a hundred years. However, without taking all factors into consideration, the results can sometimes be misleading, as was the case when explorer-archaeologist Robert Marx was searching for Columbus' lost ships, the *Capitana* and the *Santiago.*

In April, 1502, Columbus sailed with four small ships from Spain on his fourth and last voyage of discovery. He intended not only to search for gold and other precious objects in the New World but also to find a strait across Central America that would give him access to the riches of the Orient. Unfortunately, this was Columbus' most dangerous and least profitable voyage. By the time he reached the Caribbean, ship-worms had so badly damaged the hulls of his small fleet that two of the vessels had to be stripped and scuttled. With the remaining two — the *Capitana* and the *Santiago* — he headed for Santo Domingo for repairs; but he barely reached St. Ann's Bay on the north coast of Jamaica before these ships gave out and he was forced to abandon them. He and his men spent a year and five days at St. Ann's Bay before being rescued. Not long after Columbus returned to Spain from this trip, he died.

In 1940 a Harvard University expedition visited the bay and charted what they believed was the area containing the two wrecks. But no one had dived at the spot until Robert Marx arrived in Jamaica in 1965 to excavate the sunken city of old Port Royal.[1]

Since Marx had this major project in progress, he was unable to obtain official sanction from the Jamaican government to investigate St. Ann's Bay for Columbus' ships. So he decided to search on Sundays, his only days off. He, his wife, and a few volunteers systematically began probing the soft silt bottom with ten-foot-long metal rods, searching for solid objects that might reveal the presence of a wreck.

On their fifth Sunday, Marx's wife struck something solid eight feet deep in the sediment. After six hours of excavation by hand and with

[1]See chapter 7.

a bucket they laid bare a beam containing tree nails (wooden pegs) of the kind that were used in old ships to fasten timbers together. As they enlarged the hole, the divers found fragments of Spanish pottery from Columbus' time and pieces of obsidian (volcanic glass), which experts identified as originating in Central America, where the explorer had stopped before he reached St. Ann's Bay. Marx found nothing else, but he was certain that he was on the track of the two lost ships.

Two years later the Jamaican government finally gave him permission to launch a more thorough investigation of the site. Marx invited the renowned physicist Dr. Harold Edgerton of the Massachusetts Institute of Technology to join in the search. Dr. Edgerton brought with him sonar equipment of his own invention that was especially designed for locating objects buried under mud or sediment.

When the sonar revealed the presence of two wrecks beneath the bottom of the bay, a core sampler was brought in. It took three hours to drive the coring tube down into the sediment with a fifty-pound sledgehammer, and removing it proved even more difficult. But in a week the divers recovered 125 ballast rocks and took some 30 cores to ten feet below the sea floor. The cores contained Venetian glass, a coral-encrusted tack, a small black bean, several ceramic shards, and fragments of bone, charcoal, and wood. The datable material was sent to the United States, England, and Spain; three months later Marx learned the results. Most of the ballast rocks had come from Central America. The bean was a type grown in Spain. Both the Venetian glass and the ceramic pottery had been in existence in Columbus' day. But according to the radio carbon-14 tests, the oak wood fragments were twelve-hundred years old! Something must have gone wrong. But new tests on other samples of the wood produced the same result. Marx consulted experts on trees and found that it was not unusual for oak trees to grow to be one thousand years old. Thus the carbon-14 dating had not been in error after all, for it was perfectly conceivable that one of Columbus' ships had been built from an oak tree that was already seven hundred years old when it was cut down and used by the ancient boatbuilders.

Historians and leading authorities on Columbus have subsequently verified Marx's discovery, and funds are presently being raised for a full-scale excavation of the site.

The Niagara had hardly left Auckland for Vancouver in June, 1940, when she struck a mine and sank in 444 feet of water with $12 million in gold bullion.

CHAPTER TWO

Great
Salvage
Feats

Salvaging wrecks is as old as sailing itself, and to describe adequately the major salvage accomplishments of the past would fill a book. But the following bear retelling, for they are among the most dramatic and difficult undertaken in modern times.

Shortly before midnight on June 18, 1940, the huge transpacific steamer *Niagara* left Auckland, New Zealand, for Vancouver, British Columbia, with stops scheduled at Los Angeles and San Francisco. In the hold, among other cargo, were 295 sealed pinewood boxes from the Bank of England containing $12 million in gold bullion.

Three and a half hours after the *Niagara* had slipped out of Waitemata Harbor under the cover of darkness, she struck a mine. No alarm bells were sounded or needed; the steamer's passengers expected the worst of this wartime journey. Without panicking they dressed and hurried up on deck. Lifeboats were readied, and when the order to abandon ship was given, the *Niagara* was already badly listing. At 5:30

A.M. on June 19, the *Niagara*'s survivors saw the great ship slip quietly beneath the waves.

At 7:30 A.M. an airplane sighted the lifeboats, and by 11:00 A.M. the 148 passengers and 203 crew members had been picked up by a rescue boat. The *Niagara* and her cargo of nearly eight tons of solid gold were under 444 feet of water — too deep for a diver to reach with conventional diving gear.

Not long afterward the Bank of England initiated salvage operations, and three Australian companies formed a syndicate to do the work. The project was headed by Captain J. P. Williams, who first had a special diving bell designed by a consulting engineer in Melbourne, Australia, for the chief diver, John Johnstone. The *Claymore,* a two-hundred-ton, thirty-eight-year-old coastal steamer, was made the salvage vessel, and early in December, 1940, the search began.

Despite her size, finding the *Niagara* was not an easy job. Her location at the time she struck the mine was known, but she had drifted for two hours before she sank. The salvagers estimated that the *Niagara* could be anywhere within a sixteen-square-mile area, which they marked with floating buoys. The *Claymore* began systematically to drag a trawl over the bottom. Shortly after the search began, the trawl caught on an underwater obstruction. The anchor was dropped and marker buoys put out. As the trawl was winched in, its cable snapped. The broken wires indicated that they had been sheared on metal, but there were no signs of paint or rust, such as the *Niagara* might have left, on the strands. Before Johnstone could dive to investigate the mysterious object, darkness fell. The next day the weather turned bad. It was December 29 before Johnstone could go down in the bell. When he reached bottom at sixty-eight fathoms, he reported by telephone that visibility was reasonably good and that he could see a large dark object that might be the wreck. As the diving bell was being brought up, it momentarily snagged in a cable. Minutes after the diver climbed out of the steel chamber, a sailor spotted a large greenish mass submerged a few feet from the *Claymore.* To everyone's horror it was recognized as a weed-covered floating mine. Johnstone climbed over the side and tried to push it away with a boathook, but it tangled in the anchor cable. The diver then cut the vessel loose from its anchor, leaving the deadly mine moored where it was until a Navy minesweeper could come and destroy it. This was just the beginning of the salvagers' problems with floating mines.

On January 31, after weeks of futile trawling, one of the trawl cables shifted from its normal parallel course to a 45-degree angle. Thinking that it had been momentarily hung up on a rock, the captain called for more speed. The *Claymore* churned ahead, but the cable only tightened until the salvage vessel ground to a halt. Anchors and buoys were again put over the side. The sounding lead was dropped seventy-four fathoms (444 feet), and it came up with paint flecks that matched the color of the *Niagara*.

In the following two days everything seemed to go wrong. Another mine almost struck the *Claymore;* then high seas prevented diving. Finally, on February 2, Johnstone went down in the diving bell and happily reported over the telephone that they had indeed found the *Niagara*. She was lying on her side in soft mud at an angle of 70 degrees. Apparently she had struck two mines, because there were two huge, widely spaced holes ripped in her hull, although otherwise she was little damaged.

The bullion room was in the heart of the ship, and the problem was how to get into it without destroying or scattering the treasure.

Johnstone studied diagrams of the ship's interior, and he made repeated dives to the wreck to explore every possible approach. Then he constructed a detailed cardboard replica of the steamer so that while he worked on the bottom, those above could follow every move as he described his progress over the underwater telephone.

Johnstone finally decided that there was only one way to get at the treasure vault. He would blast open the *Niagara* with explosives lowered on a cable from the *Claymore* and guided into place according to the directions that he would telephone back to the surface from the diving bell. The bullion room was four decks down from the top of the steamer and twenty-six feet in from the side. It would be a long, hazardous ordeal to blast through the bulkheads one by one until he reached the vault.

On April 25 heavy charges were attached to the *Niagara* and she was split open like an overripe melon. With frequent interruptions from bad weather and the need to fend off an unending fleet of drifting mines,

blasting continued for a nerve-wracking five months. The divers penetrated deeper into the wreck, blowing off plate after plate and lifting
them out with a mechanical grab that was lowered on a cable from the
salvage ship and directed by the man in the diving bell. But there was
an increasing danger that the wreck would collapse. Moreover, each
time a charge went off, the *Claymore* jumped a foot in the water, and
dishes were often broken in the galley. Before long the constant buf-
feting began to tell on the old salvage ship. Her joints loosened, her
seams opened, and her rivets began falling out. The salvagers would
sometimes have to stop and repair their vessel before continuing work.
In the wake of the explosions, dead or stunned fish frequently littered
the surface of the sea for a square mile, and at night the phosphorescent
glow of their bodies cast an eerie bluish-green light over the ocean.
When the accumulation of debris on the *Niagara*'s deck began to hinder
the salvagers' progress, it had to be removed. For three months up to
twelve loads an hour of twisted steel were hauled off by the grab and
dumped on the sea floor, until the junkpile was sixteen feet high.

Finally, on September 25, the salvagers reached the final barrier—
the door to the bullion room. Now they had to proceed with the utmost
caution. A mistake would scatter the gold, and their months of work
would be wasted. After much thought they finally decided to blast off
the door with a twelve-pound charge.

Johnstone dived down to the wreck and directed the placing of the
explosives. The crew of the *Claymore* was tense and hushed as he pushed
down the plunger, but instead of the rumble and concussion of an
underwater explosion, nothing happened.

The charge was winched up and repaired. Then Johnstone returned
to the wreck and guided the explosives into place again. This time it
worked: the door disappeared in a welter of water. But even as this final
barrier was overcome, a new problem arose. The doorway was not large
enough to admit the grab. The opening would have to be enlarged.
Carefully, five-pound charges were swung into place and detonated to
loosen individual rivets around the entrance; then the plates were
wrenched off with the grab until a hole eight and a half feet high and
four and a half feet wide had been made into the treasure room.

At 8:42 A.M. on October 13, 1941—eleven months after the salvage operation had begun—Johnstone descended in the diving bell. Minutes later he reported that visibility was poor. The grab groped around in the treasure vault, but all it released on deck was a soggy mattress and pieces of twisted steel plates.

Johnstone tried again at 12:40 P.M. He reported over the telephone that he could see a little better, but still he failed to find any bullion. Then the men aboard the *Claymore* saw Captain Williams grip the telephone receiver tightly. "Are you sure?" he almost shouted. He ordered the bell and the grab hoisted immediately.

The diving bell surfaced first. When the hatch was unscrewed, Johnstone climbed out without a word. Next came the grab, and a shout went up when the crew saw a heavy pinewood box clutched in its metal jaws. As it was dropped on deck it split open to reveal two gold ingots. The deepest and one of the most difficult treasure salvage attempts ever made was a success.

In twenty-four days of diving, from mid-October to December, the salvors brought up 277½ boxes of bullion containing 555 ingots valued at approximately $9 million.[1] Salvage experts would have considered the project successful if only half that amount had been recovered. The final day of salvage operations on the *Niagara* was a day of rejoicing for the crew of the *Claymore*, but one of horror for the rest of the world. It was December 7, 1941.

Early in 1942 Peter Keeble, the commander of a British minesweeper in the eastern Mediterranean, was drafted as a salvage officer to clear the Red Sea port of Massaua, Ethiopia, of scuttled enemy ships. Keeble's only previous experience with hard-hat diving was an early dunking off South Africa in an ill-fitting diving suit that almost ended his career. But at Massaua he learned his new trade so well that before long his remarkable salvage accomplishments earned him the rank of Lieutenant Commander, Fleet Salvage Officer for the Mediterranean.

Once, shortly after it fell to the Allies, Keeble was sent to Tripoli to clear the harbor of seven booby-trapped ships that were blockading it. While he worked, German bombers were constantly slipping in under

---

[1] The remaining ingots either fell into the soft mud of the bottom or into some equally inaccessible spot inside the wreck.

coastal radar to bomb and strafe Allied vessels trying to off-load supplies at Tripoli. Among other things, their attacks had reduced one of the quays to a bank of concrete rubble and had sunk Keeble's diving boat beside it. The boat had gone down in forty feet of water with valuable salvage equipment aboard, and Keeble wanted to refloat it without delay. Since all his divers were busy, he decided to do the job himself. An experienced petty officer and several interested soldiers agreed to man his air pump. Dragging a crane cable behind him to shackle onto the boat's slings, Keeble clambered down the steep rubble in his bulky diving suit and sank into the black water.

He had no difficulty finding the boat and attaching the cable to the slings. But at that point the comfortable hiss of his air supply suddenly ceased.

More surprised than alarmed, Keeble reached up and closed the outlet valve on his helmet to prevent losing the air already in his suit. Then he jerked his air hose four times, demanding to be hauled up. To his amazement, yards of slack hose spiraled down to pile up at his feet. Breathing with some difficulty he staggered back toward the jetty. Blocking his path was an obstacle that had not been there before. It was his air pump, lying on its side amid the rubble of the quay. Finding it on the bottom was like looking at his own tombstone.

There was no time to wonder what had happened. Encased in a heavy diving suit forty feet down, he was breathing his own exhalations of carbon dioxide, which meant he was minutes away from suffocation. Grimly he started to climb the sloping mountain of broken concrete in front of him. His lead boots slipped and sent avalanches of rubble tumbling behind him. His hands were cut by the jagged edges of broken masonry. But worst of all, sharp pains stabbed at his chest as he fought for breath.

A quarter of the way up the slope he remembered that he was still wearing his lead front and back weights, and he shook them off.

Finally surfacing, he slumped over the edge of the jetty, gasping like a fish out of water and gesturing feebly toward his face plate. When the soldiers tried to turn it in the wrong direction, Keeble summoned enough strength to force their hands in the opposite direction, unscrewing the glass plate. When the helmet window was finally opened, he gulped down huge drafts of the sweetest air he had ever tasted.

Keeble's pumpers were only slightly less shaken than he. They had set the pump on a tilted block of concrete, and as they vigorously worked the handles, it had edged forward until the whole thing tumbled off the quay into the harbor. The only person Keeble was deeply grateful to was the German pilot who had bombed the jetty into a sloping rampart of rubble that had enabled him to walk away from certain death.

The incident was closer to ending his career as a salvage officer than the commander cared to come. But later in the war, when he was called to Beirut, Lebanon, to confer with Vice Admiral Sir Bernard Rawlings about a top-secret dive that offered only the slimmest odds of survival, it was Fleet Salvage Officer Peter Keeble who decided to do the job himself. Code-named Operation X-ray, it would be one of the deepest, most dangerous dives ever made by a hard-hat diver.

The British had sunk the German submarine U-307 near Beirut in 240 feet of water. In its control room was a secret infrared device for night vision that the British wanted at all costs. To make matters more difficult, the U-307 was within range of German airfields; the device was booby-trapped and would have to be disarmed in the dark interior of the submarine; and the whole operation had to be accomplished in a few minutes before the diver succumbed to nitrogen narcosis, the rapture of the depths that robs men of their judgment.

From photographs, British engineers built a life-size mockup of the U-307's control room. For a week Keeble practiced feeling his way through it blindfolded, lowering himself through the conning tower hatch, down through the lower hatch, inching his way past simulated piping, valves, and manifolds, and groping for the reputedly cylindrical device that would be his objective. He had to know the inside of the U-boat by heart because there would be no time for mistakes. After countless trial runs he was able to find his way by touch alone, almost without thinking—and it was this ability that saved his life during the actual dive.

Meanwhile, the diving boat was fitted with a recompression chamber. This was an elliptical, hermetically sealed tank six feet long, coupled to an air compressor so that the pressure inside the tank could be built up to equal the pressure the diver endured while working deep below the surface. When a diver, ascending from great depths, can stop for long periods at different depths, the nitrogen that his body has absorbed from breathing highly compressed air goes back into solution in his bloodstream. But if he ascends swiftly, without decompression stops, the nitrogen in his system will expand rapidly into bubbles, the way bottled soda pop does when it is uncapped. An hour or two after he has surfaced, the diver will be convulsed with excruciating pain from what is commonly called the bends, a sickness that may kill or permanently cripple him. But if the diver makes a quick ascent and then spends several hours in a recompression chamber on the surface, the pressure in the chamber can be decreased gradually to allow the nitrogen to dissolve in the diver's bloodstream without causing ill effects.

Since Keeble would be diving twice as deep as he ever had before, he knew he would be a candidate for the recompression chamber. There would be no time for decompression stops on his way up.

When everything was ready, the commander, his diving assistants, and a scientist boarded their salvage vessel *Prince Salvor* and went in search of the U-307. A day's run from Beirut put them in the general region of the sinking. Then they began a systematic search, dragging a sweep across the bottom and watching the fathometer's stylus trace the uneven contours of the sea floor on its graph.

At the end of an all-night search, the spidery line of the graph suddenly jumped up, leveled out, and dropped down again over something unusual on the bottom. As the sweep's cables tightened on the object, anchors and buoys were dropped. *Prince Salvor*'s armed escort vessels silently patroled the sea nearby, while three Spitfires circled overhead. When the salvage vessel was properly positioned over the target, Keeble climbed into his diving suit and was slowly lowered through water that gradually turned from green to gray to blue-gray, and then to the blue-black silent world 240 feet down.

His lead boots struck something solid. Peering down, he realized that he had landed on the edge of the U-boat's bridge gundeck. Cautiously he moved around the antiaircraft mounting and squeezed between the after periscope standard and a side of the bridge. The conning tower loomed before him, its brass hatch wide open. Keeble stared at the ominous black opening with some trepidation, noting its remarkable resemblance to the entrance of a tomb, which in fact it was. His most unnerving thought was that the hatchway might be booby-trapped.

Momentarily he paused, trying to slow his breathing and shake off the chill that penetrated even his heavy clothing. Then he gingerly stepped into the hatchway and began pulling himself down the ladder. His front and back weights—ninety pounds of lead—jammed against the rim of the hatch and Keeble welcomed the excuse to go no farther. On closer observation, however, he found that the hatch was oval and that by judiciously squirming and turning, he could slip the weights through.

The effort of getting inside the tower left Keeble panting for breath. The harder he breathed the less air he seemed to get. Skyrockets were going off before his eyes and he had to force himself to breathe normally. He started down the ladder again when his foot met something soft. He tried without success to stamp through it. Then, in the inky darkness, he worked the obstruction around until he straddled it. At first he thought it was a mattress; then he found a zipper, which he opened. Inside, his cold-numbed fingers touched the metal buttons of a uniform. A dead German was wedged in the conning tower.

Keeble wasted precious minutes trying to remove the corpse, but it would not give way. Finally, in nauseous desperation, he took out his heavy knife and cut his way through.

Keeble then pulled himself down through the lower hatch and into the U-boat's control room. He was swept by another wave of nausea accompanied by exploding lights and dizzyness. He knew that his time was running out. Briefly he rested near the forward periscope and tried to visualize the model of the U-boat's layout. He started in the direction he thought he was supposed to go, but after a few shuffling paces he realized that he had forgotten to count his steps. In his panic the whole sub seemed to be reeling. Then he touched the vent levers and knew where he was. The levers were back, indicating that the vents were open. Thinking that the U-boat might be salvaged one day, Keeble shoved all the levers forward and wondered why he could not hear the thump of their closing. Then he realized that he was wasting time. He had the greatest difficulty keeping his eyes open, and drowsily he wondered why it had taken so long for the "rapture" to hit him. Somewhere in the dreamlike void he heard a faint, unfamiliar voice speaking to him.

He strained to hear it, dimly aware that it had been speaking all along but that he had not been listening. It was his chief diver at the other end of the telephone telling him that it was time to come up; that it was long past time for him to come up. Keeble responded by hitting his chin switch that would buzz the topside receiver, letting them know that he had heard and understood. He did not feel like talking, and most of all he did not want them bothering him.

He dragged himself on, past the chart table and a steel partition, until he felt the junction box exactly where it had been in the mockup. He followed the main metal-sheathed cable until his hands closed on the device he had been sent to get. His fingers glided over the fastenings, the screws, the studs, the nuts, and he almost smiled. He took a screwdriver from his tool pouch and tried to guide it into the slotted head with his stiff, fumbling fingers. Then the screwdriver slipped from his grasp and disappeared. Since he was unable to bend down and pick it up, he went at the fastenings with a pair of pliers and a wrench. As he battled the seemingly endless nuts, bolts, and screws, something began to tap the back of his helmet. Keeble ignored it the first few times, but then it became distracting. Angrily he turned to feel around for whatever it was. His hand closed on a man's arm. The commander's temper cooled quickly but he was not overly surprised or shocked. He felt the puffy hand with a thick ring on one finger and knew that that was what had been hitting his helmet. He pushed the drifting body away and went back to work.

After what seemed like an eternity, the last troublesome nut gave way and he had the prize. By then his hands were well lacerated, he had broken or lost a number of his tools, and he was too exhausted to cheer, even mentally.

Numbed by fatigue but with a firm grip on the sensing device, he groped his way back through the control room. At the bottom of the ladder he gasped a request into his telephone for a weighted bag on a line.

The chief diver replied that the bag was on its way, that he was long overdue, and that another diver was coming down to help.

Infuriated, Keeble croaked out that they should hold their blasted diver. The nitrogen was getting to him.

He climbed back out of the conning tower, placed the sensing device in the waiting bag, and asked to be hauled up.

After several hours in the recompression chamber, a shower, and a rest, Keeble talked to the scientist who had been sent along to examine the secret device.

"Was it all right?" Keeble asked. "I didn't bring up the wardroom clock by mistake?"

"Perfectly all right," the scientist replied, beaming. "But what puzzles me is how you managed to short-circuit the demolition charge without touching it off. The contacts were closed, but—"

"The demolition charge!" exclaimed Keeble. "Christ! I forgot all about it!"

The commander of the Monitor *(in white hat) inspects the minor damage that his ship sustained during her engagement with the Confederate ironclad* Merrimac.

CHAPTER THREE

The

Missing

Monitor

One of the most unusual vessels to end its existence in the "Graveyard of the Atlantic" was the famous federal gunboat the *Monitor*. She was the first of the Union's ironclads, a radically new, strange-looking craft 172 feet long with a 41-foot beam, a $7\frac{1}{2}$-foot draft, and a weight of 776 tons. From a distance all that showed above water was a small wheelhouse on her bow and a twenty-foot-diameter, nine-foot-high revolving gunport encased in armor eight inches thick and housing two eleven-inch Dahlgren cannons. Since so little of the ironclad was visible at sea, she was graphically nicknamed a cheesebox on a raft.

The *Monitor* gained fame for her only naval engagement when she fought the Confederate ironclad *Merrimac* off Hampton Roads, Virginia, on March 9, 1862. Nine months later, on December 29, 1862, the *Monitor* left Hampton Roads under tow by the federal paddle-wheeler *Rhode Island* to join the Union blockade of Wilmington, North Carolina.

On the afternoon of the next day, the two vessels encountered gale winds off Cape Hatteras. The waves began breaking over the *Monitor*'s pilothouse and turret. By 8:00 P.M. the ironclad was pitching dangerously. Under the sea's constant pounding the oakum packing loosened in a seam around the base of the gun turret. The "cheesebox on a raft" began taking water faster than her pumps could handle it. When the captain realized that there was no hope for his vessel, he lit a red distress lantern indicating that he was abandoning ship and he requested boats from the *Rhode Island* to transfer his crew. The paddle-wheeler dropped the tow line, but it fouled in one of the wheels. Two small boats were launched from the *Rhode Island* and slowly made their way through the stormy sea toward the foundering ironclad.

In an attempt to stabilize his ship, the *Monitor*'s skipper dropped anchor so that the vessel would point into the wind. By 11:30 P.M., with great difficulty, only one of the rescue boats managed to maneuver close enough to the wallowing gunboat to take off some of her crew. The deck of the ironclad was now completely submerged. Before the rescue boat could approach again, the *Monitor* began to drag her anchor and drifted off into the darkness, where she sank with sixteen men still aboard.

Over the next ninety-two years many attempts were made to locate the remains of the famous gunboat, but the shifting sands of the Graveyard guarded their secret well. The exact resting place of the *Monitor* remained a mystery until July, 1955. At that time a twenty-one-year-old Marine from Camp Lejeune, North Carolina, found the *Monitor*. His name was Robert Marx, and the story of his fascinating search is described in detail in *Diving for Pleasure and Treasure* by Clay Blair, Jr. (World Publishing Company, 1960).

Marx was a young man with a passion for two things: historical research and diving. Both were well served on the very coast where he was stationed. He spent every weekend roaming the bleak beaches of Cape Hatteras, skin diving offshore, visiting the local museums, and talking with people. Everyone along the Outer Banks had some tale to tell about the shipwrecks, but the one that intrigued Marx most was the story of the missing *Monitor*. He decided to try to find the famous ironclad.

Instead of spending weekends at the coast, Marx began devoting his free time to maritime museums and libraries. At the National Archives in Washington, D.C., he read the log of the *Rhode Island*, paying particular attention to the eyewitness reports and noting with interest that no one ever saw the *Monitor* actually sink. Therefore, he saw no reason to believe the general assumption that she was ten miles or even twenty-five miles from shore.

In 1954 Marx met an old Outer Banker who showed him a family record book with the notation that early in January, 1865, two years after the *Monitor* had sunk, the family had held a picnic on the beach near the Cape Hatteras lighthouse, where they had seen the "Yankee cheesebox on a raft" in the breakers.

The clue excited Marx. He wondered if the present lighthouse had been standing in the same place all these years. He checked and found that it had not. But the foundation to the old one was still visible only one hundred feet away. He took a week's leave, lugged his scuba gear to the beach, and began a systematic but fruitless search of the breakers.

In the course of further research, he found an old map of Cape Hatteras that showed the lighthouse even further from the water's edge than the old foundation. Marx wondered whether he had the right lighthouse. If he did, erosion had so eaten at the shore that the breakers and the *Monitor* the old-timers had seen would have been at least a mile out from the present shoreline. Other old records revealed that the bodies of five of the *Monitor*'s crew had washed ashore after the wreck and were buried on a knoll beside a cedar tree half a mile behind the lighthouse.

Marx found the knoll on private property. The tree was now only a rotted cedar stump, and beside it was a large hole. He climbed into the hole and was looking around when an old man with a rifle slipped up behind him and accused him of trespassing. Marx started to explain that he was only looking for evidence that would help him locate the *Monitor*.

"What's the *Monitor?*" the old man asked.

Marx felt that if he did not know, there was no sense in explaining.

"Come up to the house for a drink," the old man said, and turning, he led the perplexed Marx to a weather-beaten clapboard house overlooking the old lighthouse foundation.

To his astonishment, Marx saw on the wall of the living room a map of Cape Hatteras. On it in bright red grease pencil was written the word

"Monitor" with an X offshore where Marx thought the wreck might be. A nearby bookcase contained at least two dozen books dealing with the *Monitor.*

Now Marx was more confused than ever. Had the old man dug up the grave? Why had he acted as if he did not know what the *Monitor* was? Marx tried to work the conversation around to his favorite subject, but the old man refused to discuss it. Marx left the house a little later feeling somewhat uneasy.

Not long afterward a friend told him that the old man was a kind of journalist and amateur historian whose hobby was the *Monitor.* Marx made a point of meeting him again, and this time the old man told him everything he had learned about the ironclad. He said he thought the wreck lay offshore a mile from the lighthouse. He had inspected the area many times from his airplane and believed that nine times in seven years he had spotted the old hulk and obtained rough bearings on it.

But he had seen the wreck only when conditions were ideal, he told Marx. First, the water had to be perfectly still and clear, a rare condition for Cape Hatteras. Next, the plane had to be at an altitude of eleven hundred or twelve hundred feet, with the sun shining from behind as it flew toward the beach. That was the only way he had ever seen the *Monitor.*

Marx and the old man conducted a number of joint searches, the former in a boat, the latter in his plane, but the water was never right.

Long after Marx and the old man parted ways, the Marine stubbornly kept up the air-sea search with several friends who owned a plane. Finally, one morning in June, 1955, as the plane was aloft and Marx was riding a rubber life raft in the swells watching for the pilot to dip his wings when something was sighted, the plane suddenly buzzed him, waggling its wings furiously. It repeated the maneuver several times until Marx thought his friends had gone crazy. Slipping into the water he towed the life raft ashore as the airplane landed on the highway. His two friends climbed out breathless with excitement.

"Marx! Marx!" they yelled. "You can see wrecks all over the place. Get up there! You can see the *Monitor.* Close in by shore."

The Marine boarded the plane; the pilot climbed to twelve hundred feet and then swung in toward shore. Marx later related: "It was one of those rare days when the water was as calm as a millpond and you could see clear to the bottom. We flew over the area, and as I looked down I could see at least a dozen wrecks scattered about like toy ships in the bottom of a bathtub. I told Holland [the pilot] to fly over the spot where the *Monitor* was supposed to be and, sure enough, there she was. I could see the gun turret and the little pilot house sticking up on the bow. The stern was half buried in sand."

The pilot made repeated passes over the wreck so that Marx could drop a lard-can marker attached to a cement block anchor. But his aim was poor and the marker landed a hundred yards inshore of the *Monitor.*

Back on the beach a series of unfortunate circumstances prevented Marx from making an immediate dive. One of his companions had a serious accident and had to be rushed to the hospital. The next day, despite bad weather and the rough seas, Marx tried to reach the site in a small outboard motorboat. It nearly swamped before he was forced back. For the next four days he sat on the beach watching helplessly as his buoy bobbed in the distance. Finally his leave expired and he had to return to Camp Lejeune without diving on the long-lost *Monitor.*

News of Marx's discovery reached the press, and *Life* magazine decided to sponsor him for a return expedition. To help with the diving, Marx asked Keith Ingram, a twenty-five-year-old Marine lieutenant, to join him. They chartered a sixty-four-foot boat with a fathometer and headed for the waters off the lighthouse.

Marx's buoy had long since drifted away, but he still had rough bearings on the wreck that he had taken from the air. Since this left considerable room for error, they plotted an area a mile square around this point and methodically began scanning the bottom with the depth finder. The characteristic lump they were looking for that would indicate the wreck eluded them for several days. Finally a United States Coast and Geodetic Survey ship with superior sounding equipment joined the search. Six hours later the sonar operator made contact with a metallic object on the bottom and dropped a marker.

Early the next morning Marx dived down to check it. He found bottom at forty-three feet. Visibility was five or six feet. A short distance from the marker line he saw a troughlike formation in the ocean floor that he knew indicated hidden wreckage. As he swam along it, he sud-

TEXT CONTINUED ON PAGE 52

A contemporary news drawing, below, shows the Monitor *being launched less than four months after construction began. The cutaway side and bird's-eye views of the ship (opposite) reveal the innovative swivel turret, which allowed the Union gunners to fire the ironclad's two cannon in any direction except directly over the bow, where they were blocked by the four-foot-high pilot-house. Opposite, below, the* Monitor's *crew poses by the turret after the long but inconclusive artillery duel with the* Merrimac.

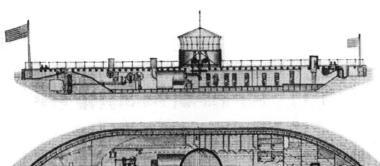

denly came upon the *Monitor*'s gun turret sticking up about three feet out of the sand. Excitedly he circled it, noting its gunports and the large rivets spaced around the top of the armor plating. Then he swam down the trough again, estimating its dimensions. When he was certain of his identification, he surfaced and shouted the news to the others.

Marx climbed aboard and exchanged his air tank for one he had used briefly the day before but had set aside because he said the air was foul. He and Ingram then dived to see if they could attach a buoy line to the turret. Minutes later on the bottom, Marx suddenly became dizzy. A pain shot through his body, and as he said later, "My air tasted like rubber." He spit out his mouthpiece and surfaced quickly.

Marx was pulled aboard dazed and half conscious. Moments later Ingram returned and said he had swum over the turret and had seen it clearly, sticking out of the sand.

By the time they got Marx out of his diving rig and onto a bunk, the sea had grown rough and a rain squall had moved in. The boat had already swung off its position, but the crew took a fix with a sextant anyway. In a few minutes Marx was back on his feet, determined to place a marker on the turret. Against everyone's better judgment he dived again with Ingram, but a moment later he surfaced with a violent headache.

After a while Ingram returned with the disappointing news that he had been unable to find the turret. The boat had put out two hundred feet of anchor chain and had apparently moved well away from the wreck. But the divers were not unduly alarmed because they felt they had a good sextant fix on the spot.

The boat returned to port and waited a day for a *Life* photographer to arrive. Marx, complaining of a lingering earache, was advised by a doctor to suspend all diving for a while. He took the news hard.

The following morning Ingram and the photographer dived to take pictures of the wreck. Visibility was less than six feet, the currents were bad, and they were unable to find the *Monitor*. Marx paced the deck impatiently. Repeatedly the divers searched the bottom but failed to find the wreck.

Three weeks later another attempt was made with the assistance of Navy frogmen. This too failed. How was it possible to miss a target the

TEXT CONTINUED ON PAGE 56

The most serious casualty in the battle between the Monitor and the Merrimac was the Union ship's commander, Lieutenant John L. Worden, shown here wearing glasses after the fight. He was at the wheel when a shell exploded at the eye slit of the pilothouse, sending flames and powder grains into his eyes and forcing him to turn over command of the ship to one of his subordinates. OVERLEAF: The four-hour battle of the ironclads was the subject of many pictures. This rendition was made in 1862, the year in which the two ships clashed off Norfolk, Virginia.

size of the *Monitor*'s gun turret, which protruded three feet out of the bottom and was twenty feet in diameter?

The probable answers to the mystery were worked out weeks after the last expedition. By the time bearings were taken, the boat had probably swung well away from the wreck on its two-hundred-foot anchor chain. Also, the depth of the water off Cape Hatteras changes frequently as the sand sweeps back and forth over the bottom. Three-foot changes are not unusual, and after a storm, ten-to-twenty-foot shifts have been recorded.

Somewhere off Cape Hatteras the *Monitor* still awaits rediscovery. Perhaps one day the sands of the Graveyard will shift again, the sea will subside, and in that one clear, rare moment, someone will again see the "Yankee cheesebox on a raft."

The Monitor *was under tow by the paddle-wheeler* Rhode Island *(in the background) from Hampton Roads to Wilmington, North Carolina, when a storm struck. The tow line was released, and although boats from the* Rhode Island *managed to take off some of the* Monitor's *crewmen, sixteen were lost.*

Havana was an important way station for homeward bound Spanish treasure fleets.

CHAPTER FOUR

The

Doomed

Armada

ednesday, July 24, 1715, was warm and muggy despite the gentle sea breeze that rippled the cobalt-blue waters of Havana harbor. Aboard his flagship, General Juan Estéban Ubilla, commander of the *Flota*, surveyed the armada that awaited only his signal to sail for Spain. There were eleven vessels in all, including the French ship *Grifòn*, which had gained permission to accompany the fleet for her own safety. Five of the galleons, under the command of General Antonio de Echeverz, were laden with the wealth of South America—gold, emeralds, and pearls from Cartagena, Colombia, and Peruvian silver loaded at Portobelo, Panama. Ubilla's five galleons contained the wealth of Mexico—2,290 chests of newly minted silver and gold coins from Veracruz, as well as delicate porcelains and silks from China, and an assortment of exquisite gem-studded jewelry secretly ordered by King Philip for his new bride, the seductive Elizabeth Farnese, Duchess of Parma. The total treasure amounted to more than 14 million pesos[1] and was destined for the royal coffers of Spain. It was one of the largest shipments ever made, for the treasure fleets had been delayed two years by the War of the Spanish Succession, which had embroiled half of Europe.

General Ubilla shifted his gaze away from the ships to look again at the sea and the sky, hoping some sign would tell him what the weather would bring in the next few days while the fleet passed through the treacherous Florida Straits. All he saw were fleecy white clouds drifting across a calm azure emptiness. But Ubilla was not so easily reassured. It was already past mid-July, and he knew the risks of sailing late, the penalty for being caught between reef and shoals in adverse weather. The old Caribbean jingle that warned of hurricanes was not to be taken lightly. "June, too soon; July, stand by; August, come they must; September, remember; October, all over."

Ubilla murmured an invocation, asking a blessing on his fleet that it might safely weather the long, perilous journey ahead. Then, turning brusquely away from the rail, he gave the order to set sail.

A brass cannon aboard the flagship relayed the command to the armada. An answering salute thundered from the grim walls of El Morro fortress. Suddenly the fleet came to life. Bare feet pounded the decks as the crews worked creaking block and tackle. Hawsers strummed as the huge anchors were lifted to the accompaniment of clanking capstan pawls. Billows of white canvas blossomed from fore, main, and mizzenmasts, flapping and luffing until yardarms were hauled around and halyards made fast. Then the sails caught the breeze and filled. The galleons lumbered forward slowly, awkwardly, led by Ubilla's and de Echeverz's flagships, the *Capitanas,* one-thousand-ton giant men-of-war armed with tiers of iron cannon. Behind them came the heavily laden merchant *naos,* flanked by the lighter, sloop-rigged *urcas* and the swift patrol *pataches.* Bringing up the rear were the two huge, seven-hundred-ton, sixty-gun *Almirantas,* the fighting galleons of each fleet.

Gradually the vessels gained speed and heeled heavily as they plowed into the pull of the Gulf Stream, their stubby bows pointed toward the

[1]Whether made of gold or silver, a peso was a monetary unit equivalent to thirteen reals (coins). Reals were minted in the following denominations: 8, 4, 2, 1, $\frac{1}{2}$.

distant Florida Keys. The long-awaited Spanish treasure fleet of 1715 was finally under way, set on a disaster course that had already destined it for a rendezvous with modern history.

Monday, July 29. In the distance to the leeward of the armada lies the low Florida coast, but even in the midday sun a strange milky haze obscures the view. The sea looks like a polished emerald, but the galleons begin to roll on long steady swells sweeping toward shore. The members of the crew who claim they can "feel" the coming of bad weather in their bones complain of aching joints. General Ubilla says nothing to his officers, but they notice that he is spending more time than usual on deck, staring to the east. A young cabin boy aboard de Echeverz's *Almiranta* is amazed at the great number of fish he sees in the water, more than he has seen during the entire voyage from Spain. But when he excitedly calls this to the attention of some of the older seamen, they act as if they neither see the fish nor hear what the boy has said. By Monday night the prevailing easterly wind has slackened noticeably.

Tuesday, July 30. Dawn breaks on an oppressively hot, humid day. The seamen's clothes stick to their bodies. The wind is erratic, sometimes changing directions abruptly, sometimes ceasing to blow at all. During these lulls the creaking rigging of distant galleons is easily heard over the water. The sun seems enveloped in thin yellowish gauze. The unceasing swells grow larger and the galleons roll with more abandon. By noon there is not a man or boy in the entire fleet who does not know that there is grave trouble ahead.

Gradually the wind picks up out of the northwest. The galleons lean into the steepening swells. Shreds of grayish clouds skim across the sky, gathering in an ominous black mantle that blots out the sun. By midafternoon it grows so dark that stern lanterns must be lighted. The wind, increasing to twenty knots, moans through halyards and shrouds. With a hissing rush, a wall of rain advances on the fleet, the wind-driven drops hammering the foaming seas so hard that they seem to smoke. Deck hands claw forward to secure hatches, shielding their faces against the stinging fury of the squall. Then the rain passes as quickly as it came. But the wind moves into the north-northeast and blows harder, gusting to thirty knots. Mountainous waves crash over the bows. Officers and men alike strain to see the arcing amber glow of lanterns on the vessels

TEXT CONTINUED ON PAGE 64

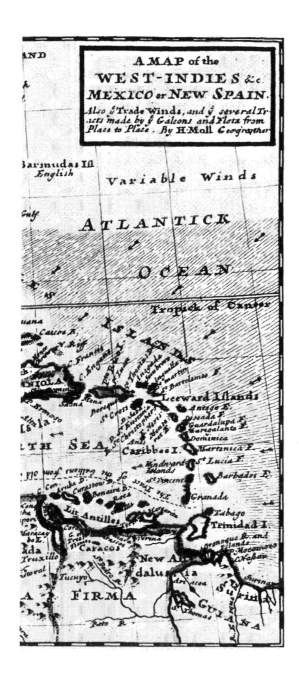

A MAP of the
WEST-INDIES &c.
MEXICO or NEW SPAIN.
Also ẙ Trade Winds, and ẙ several Tr-
.acts made by ẙ Galeons and Flota from
Place to Place. By H.Moll Geographer

This map was drawn barely a dozen years after the Spanish treasure fleet of 1715 met its ill-starred end on the east coast of Florida. The cartographer has clearly indicated the routes that the Spanish galleons took to Havana and then homeward.

ahead as the specks of light rise, lurch, and fall, tracing eerie patterns in the darkness. Generals Ubilla and de Echeverz know that the worst is yet to come and that they cannot turn back. Their only hope is to go on, to try to pass Cape Canaveral and the last of the treacherous reefs to their leeward before they are caught in the full force of the hurricane.

By midnight the fleet has been pounded by five vicious squalls, each worse than the one before. Sails and rigging are showing the strain. Foresails and mains have long since been reefed, but the topsail of General de Echeverz's *Almiranta* is swept away in the storm. The crews are exhausted by the fight to control careening yardarms and repair broken halyards.

2:00 A.M., *Wednesday, July 31.* The hurricane strikes with winds up to one hundred miles an hour. Officers scream orders that go unheard in the unearthly howling, the ripping of sails, the sickening crash of splintered masts. Every ship is on its own now, and those that are not immediately disabled try desperately to gain sea room, to beat their way away from the jagged reefs. But on each vessel there is pandemonium. Decks are littered with terror-stricken men struggling to free themselves from falling rigging. Straining to avoid the reefs, some of the galleons lose headway and broach to the mountainous waves that swamp them amidships, engulfing crew and wreckage. Other ships, completely demasted, flounder; towering waves quickly sweep away every living thing. Destruction is swift and complete; the loss of lives is appalling.

General Ubilla's *Capitana* is disemboweled from stem to stern on the first reef it strikes. Ballast, cargo, cannon, and treasure tumble out through the gaping hole in its hull as the ship pitches onto a second reef that totally demolishes it. The general and 225 of his men perish.

General de Echeverz's *Capitana* is caught broadside by the storm and sinks a short distance from a point of land. Although the beach is little more than a stone's throw away, the general and 113 others are either dashed to death on the rocks or drowned. De Echeverz's *Almiranta, Nuestra Señora de Rosario y San Francisco Xavier,* breaks up under the weight of the waves. His merchant ship and sloop are swallowed by the sea, never to be found. Two of the patrol vessels, the *Santa Christo del*

Valle y Nuestra Señora de la Concepción and *Nuestra Señora de las Nieves y las Ánimas,* are literally torn apart in the rampaging surf. On one, 135 persons perish; on the other, the crew is more fortunate. Although two dozen drown as the deck lifts off the hull, some 100 survivors ride the wreckage ashore like a raft. Ubilla's *Almiranta* sinks in shallow water within wading distance of the beach, but pounding waves rapidly demolish it, and 125 persons are battered to death before they can reach shore. *La Holandesa,* a merchant *nao,* is cast up high and dry by the hurricane; the crew miraculously escapes without a fatality. Ubilla's sloop, *Nuestra Señora de la Regla,* runs aground at the mouth of a river; 35 crewmen survive.

The terrible hurricane of 1715 has taken its toll in a matter of minutes. Of the eleven vessels in the fleet, only one survives—the French ship *Grifòn,* whose captain, Don Antonio Darié, was sailing farthest to the northeast when the hurricane struck. In an incredible feat of seamanship, Darié forced his vessel into the wind and managed to avoid being swept onto the reefs. The other ten ships, 14 million pesos of registered treasure, and one thousand lives were lost in one of the worst sea disasters of all time.

For those who survived—and old records report that some one thousand made it ashore near Sebastian Inlet—the nightmare was far from over. In the early morning hours the hurricane moved inland. Dawn broke to reveal wreckage and bodies tumbling in the surf and littering the beaches. Those who had survived the night clustered together in isolated groups, doing what they could for the seriously injured. There were no nearby towns, and no medicine, food, or tools had been salvaged. Many who survived the worse ordeals of the night died from their injuries the next morning. Gradually, however, the gales subsided, the seas grew less violent, and officers restored order.

The closest settlement was St. Augustine—150 miles to the north. Few wanted to strike inland because the wilderness was inhabited by fierce tribes of Indians. Finally it was decided that the bulk of the group would establish a camp on the beach out of salvage from the wreckage, while a small party would attempt to reach St. Augustine in two longboats that had washed ashore virtually undamaged. Still others saw an immediate opportunity to enrich themselves. Risking whatever dangers

TEXT CONTINUED ON PAGE 68

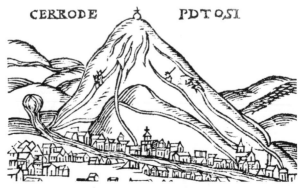

CERRO DE   POTOSI

The silver mines at Potosí, Bolivia (left), were first exploited in 1545. The veins proved to be so rich that by the beginning of the seventeenth century Potosí was the world's largest single source of silver, and with a population of 160,000, the biggest town in the New World. When silver from this and other mines in Peru and Mexico was loaded onto Spanish ships, it naturally attracted covetous seafarers from every nation. Above, a contemporary engraving shows a Dutch force successfully attacking a Spanish treasure fleet off Cuba in 1628. At the right are silver coins minted by the Spaniards during the 1500's.

awaited them inland, they filled their pockets with treasure and set off on foot for St. Augustine.

Late in the first week of August, the first of the survivors struggled into Saint Augustine. For days they had traveled by boat and had then walked a great distance overland. When they arrived they were half naked, half starved, and badly in need of medical attention. The Spanish settlement was stunned by the tragedy. A report of the disaster was quickly dispatched to Spain and Havana with a request that a rescue party be sent to Sebastian Inlet. Meanwhile, guards were posted along Matanzas Inlet south of St. Augustine to intercept the treasure-laden deserters. Those who were caught were executed.

Six weeks later, in September, seven rescue ships arrived at Sebastian Inlet and picked up the last survivors.

When Spain learned the fate of her long-awaited treasure fleet, a royal order was sent to Cuba instructing the Sergeant Major of Havana, Don Juan de Hoyo Solórzano, to commence salvage operations at once — an order more easily given than executed in the early eighteenth century. Official word to begin work probably did not arrive in Havana for at least three or four months. Even then, the task of obtaining seaworthy ships and recruiting crews for an extended stay away from home port usually took three to five months to execute. Solórzano apparently wasted no time. Early Spanish historians reported that he crossed the Florida Straits six months later with several sloops guided by some of the survivors and arrived at the wreck site in March, 1716.

Solórzano found that not only had the treasure ships been gutted by the reefs, but they had been battered so badly that the valuable cargo was strewn over a wide area of the ocean floor. The water along this coast was not clear, and six months of constant pummeling by surf and tide had already covered much of the wreckage with a thin layer of sand.

But the salvage problem was not Solórzano's only worry. The Florida Straits southward into the Caribbean were the hunting ground of privateers who considered unescorted treasure galleons the plumpest of game. This was why the Spanish flota, or fleet system, had come about. Few pirate ships were foolhardy enough to tackle these heavily armed armadas single-handedly. But to raid a lightly armed salvage ship intent on scooping up the treasure of an entire fleet was something else again.

Realizing this, Solórzano first established a fortified camp and storehouse about two and one half miles south of Sebastian Inlet, opposite one of the shipwrecked galleons.

Salvage operations in the eighteenth century were tediously slow but surprisingly effective considering the primitive equipment. Moreover, Solórzano had more than 280 Indian divers at his disposal. These men were expert swimmers trained to hold their breath from three to five minutes underwater. They functioned in relay teams, some divers clutching heavy stones to hurry their descent to the bottom while others brought down ropes from the salvage vessel. Once amid the wreckage, the divers felt around until they located something of value, then surfaced with it. If it was too heavy to lift, such as a chest of silver, the ropes were attached and the object hauled up from above. Eyewitnesses mention that Solórzano also used "diving engines." These were diving bells of the crudest kind, usually no more than inverted wooden tubs that trapped air inside them as they were lowered to the bottom. Whenever an exhausted diver needed a breath, he could duck under one of these "diving engines" without taking the time to return to the surface. And time was something that Solórzano could not afford to lose. With one eye cocked for pirates, he undoubtedly drove his divers unmercifully, for of his 280 Indians, more than a third died from drowning and other causes. Life was cheap; Spanish time and treasure were not.

The accumulated treasure was taken ashore and put in the guarded storehouse. When the total amounted to 4 million pesos of silver, it was loaded aboard a ship and dispatched to Havana. Surprisingly, the shipment got through without being intercepted by any of the marauders of the Spanish Main. But Solórzano's luck was wearing thin. Word of the lost treasure and the Spaniards' frantic salvage efforts had already reached the infamous pirate stronghold at Port Royal, Jamaica, where a number of rogues were planning some salvage operations of their own. As luck would have it, however, a respected gentleman in Virginia named Captain Henry Jennings was one jump ahead of them.

Jennings was an English privateer commissioned as were others of his day to use privately owned war vessels to prey upon enemy shipping. Between wars, privateers were supposed to suppress piracy. The Treaty of Utrecht, signed two years earlier, had established peace between England and Spain. But Jennings was not a man to let such a trivial matter as a peace treaty stand in his way. When he sailed from Williamsburg, Virginia, with five ships, three hundred men, and a directive from Virginia's Governor Spotswood to "see what was about," the suppression of piracy was not exactly what the daring privateer had in mind.

According to an account published in 1724, Jennings sailed his fleet directly to the salvage site in Florida, landed his three hundred well-armed men, and attacked the Spanish camp. After a short skirmish, he overran sixty guards at the storehouse and made off with 350,000 pesos of silver. With this much booty aboard there was no longer any thought of returning to the comparatively respectable life of a privateer. He sailed to Port Royal and took up the career of a pirate.

So far as is known, Captain Jennings never paid for his crimes as a pirate, avoiding the gallows by shrewdly quitting when he was ahead. Three years after plundering the Spanish treasure, he appeared in Nassau, in the Bahama Islands, when the king's pardon was granted there to any pirates who cared to surrender. Later he retired to Bermuda to lead a life of complete respectability, made more bearable, perhaps, with the help of several chests of Spanish silver.

Captain Jennings' successful raid on the Spanish salvage site was encouraging news to every cutthroat on the Spanish Main. No one ever duplicated the feat in such magnitude, but there were many who profited in a less spectacular way from the Spanish misfortune. Pirates far and wide were attracted to the site. Although the Spaniards reinforced their operations with more armed ships and men, the area was long a favorite "fishing" ground for freebooters using rakes, grappling hooks, and divers. Although Solórzano recovered most of the easily accessible silver within months after the disaster, the Spaniards continued salvaging until 1719, almost four years after the fleet went down. Of the 14 million pesos of registered treasure that was scattered across the reefs on that fateful night in July, 1715, it is estimated that roughly 6 million was salvaged. The remaining 8 million pesos in gold and silver were destined to lie beneath the shifting sands of the Atlantic for the next 240 years, waiting for a new breed of treasure hunters to find them.

Early Spanish colonists in South America were forced to be their own shipwrights.

These Chinese porcelain bowls were salvaged from the ill-fated armada of 1715.

CHAPTER FIVE

Treasure
Trove

The first of the new kind of treasure hunters was Kip Wagner, a white-haired, scholarly looking building contractor from Ohio who knew nothing about how to search for treasure when he moved his family to the east coast of Florida at the end of World War II. Wagner had come to build a motel at Wabasso, a small town eight miles from Sebastian Inlet, where a desolate stretch of beach was to change his life forever.

Sebastian Inlet has altered little since the time of Solórzano and the early treasure hunters. It is a narrow, treacherous, rock-bound pass that empties into the Atlantic Ocean about forty miles south of Cape Kennedy. The channel is navigable at high tide, but at any other time its racing crosscurrents have spelled disaster for many an unwary yachtsman. No one knows why, but beyond the mouth of the pass, where channel waters meet the Atlantic, the seething turbulence attracts many large sharks. It is one of the few places along the coast where shark fishermen can consistently catch tiger sharks simply by letting the currents whisk their big baits out of the inlet.

South from Sebastian to Wabasso, the steep, palmetto-covered sand dunes are relatively deserted and the ocean is seldom calm. When the tide is up, it gnaws at the base of the dunes. When it is down, it exposes a one-hundred-foot-wide strip of beach. Old-timers at Sebastian and Wabasso have long claimed that the time to follow the ebb tide in search of old coins is after a particularly severe northeaster has scoured the beach. Everyone knows about the blackened, irregularly shaped coins that have appeared for years along this beach, but few people are able to produce the evidence. It is the kind of lore that fits the country. Whether the tourists believe the stories or not is of no particular concern to the old-timers.

Like any new arrival, Kip Wagner heard about the old coins when he came to Wabasso. At first he was skeptical, then he grew curious. When the weekend vacationers left, Wagner combed the beach simply to satisfy his curiosity. He never found a coin. Nor, despite the stories, could he find anyone who ever had. Still, he was reluctant to disregard the stories as pure fiction. There had to be some truth to them. Surreptitiously he tried to track down some of the more popular yarns. There was an old postmaster of Sebastian who at the turn of the century had reportedly collected a cigar box of gold and silver coins over the years. One night he was murdered, and the coins were never found. Another man, it was said, had retrieved an unusually heavy "brick" from the shallow waters. He used the brick in building a fireplace, and according to the story, the first time he lighted a fire the brick melted. Finally, Wagner came across a man in his eighties who said that he did not know what the blackened, odd-shaped pieces of metal that he had picked up along the beach were, but that they made fine "skipping stones." When Wagner asked how many he thought he had found, the old gentleman said he reckoned he had tossed some two thousand back into the ocean.

Not long afterward, Wagner visited the beach with one of his construction workers and was amazed when the man picked up seven of the black, oxidized silver coins within a half hour, and as nonchalantly gave them to souvenir hunters a short while later. Once again Wagner had failed to find a single coin. But now he knew why. They looked like nothing he had ever seen before. They resembled pieces of dirty scrap metal cut into odd shapes and ranged in size from a quarter to a silver dollar.

From that moment on Wagner was a firm believer in the tales of treasure that might be found on the beach.

It was almost a year later, however, before he found his first silver coin. He had borrowed an Army-surplus metal detector from a friend for his customary patrols along the beach. After uncovering a large number of tin cans and other junk, the detector finally led him to his first genuine piece of eight—a sea-blackened coin about the size of a silver dollar. In the weeks and months that followed, Wagner found other coins, or "cobs" as they were called by the British colonials because they were cut from a lump or bar of silver. The coins had anywhere from three to eight angular sides, hence the popular term "pieces of eight." In time, Wagner unearthed forty such coins—all stamped with the cross and arms of Spain and none dated later than 1715. Gradually Wagner narrowed his search to the base of a large bluff which seemed to produce more coins than any other area. He named the place his "money beach." Often, after a severe storm, he found as many as five coins there. But he could not say whether they were buried in the sand or whether the sea had washed them up.

The answer to this puzzling question came on the tail of a hurricane. For two days howling gales and torrential rains pounded the coast. When the storm finally passed, Wagner hurried to his money beach to find it completely altered. The waves had undermined the dunes and chewed terraces into the beach, which was now two feet deep in debris. Sites where he had found coins before were now completely gone. Wagner dejectedly kicked his way through the clusters of driftwood and seaweed for a closer look at the beach. Suddenly he spotted an eight-sided piece of silver. The coin was dated 1714. There was little doubt now where it had come from. The Atlantic waves had wrenched it off the bottom and deposited it on shore along with all the other flotsam and jetsam from the storm. Wagner was now convinced that a tremendous treasure was waiting to be found in the heaving gray sea washing at his feet.

Armed with an inner tube and a homemade face mask, he began searching offshore, but found nothing that even vaguely resembled a shipwreck. All the coins that anyone had ever found had been minted before 1715, so there had to be a record somewhere of a shipwreck occurring in the area in that year. Wagner and an enthusiastic friend, Dr. Kip G. Kelso, read every book they could find about early wrecks. When they had exhausted the books in the public library, they moved on to the Florida University Library, then to other libraries in distant cities. Meanwhile, someone told Wagner that a Spanish fleet, loaded with some 14 million pesos worth of gold and silver, had been hit by a hurricane in 1715 and had gone down near what was then Cape Canaveral.

Wagner sent his 1714 coin to the Smithsonian Institution and asked if it could have come from the 1715 treasure fleet. A Smithsonian expert wrote back that this was impossible since the fleet had been sunk 150 miles farther south in the Florida Keys, and he was presently writing a book about it.

Despite the disappointingly conflicting reports, Kelso went to Washington, D.C., to research the archives of the Library of Congress. After days of intensive reading, he stumbled onto a major piece of evidence that substantiated everything the treasure hunters had suspected. In a book called *A Concise Natural History of East and West Florida,* written by the English cartographer Bernard Romans and published in 1775, Kelso found this statement: "Directly opposite the mouth of San Sebastian River happened the shipwreck of the Spanish Admiral, who was the northermost wreck of fourteen galleons, and a hired Dutch ship, all laden with specie and plate; which by [undistinguishable word] of northeast winds were drove ashore and lost on this coast, between this place and the bleech-yard, in 1715. A hired Frenchman, fortunately escaped, by having steered half a point more east than the others. The people employed in the course of our survey, while walking the strand after strong eastern gales, have repeatedly found pistareens and double pistareen, which kinds of money probably yet remaining in the wrecks. This lagoon stretches parallel to the sea, until the latitude 27:20, where it has an outwatering, or mouth. Directly before this mouth, in three fathom water, lie the remains of the Dutch wreck. The banks of this lagoon are not fruitful."

Kelso could hardly believe his good fortune. Not only was this documented evidence of the wrecks written just sixty years after the fatal hurricane, but Romans had included in the book's flyleaf a highly detailed map. When Kelso examined the Sebastian Inlet area with a magnifying glass, he read Romans' notation: "Opposite this River, perished, the Admiral, commanding the Plate Fleet 1715, the rest of the fleet, 14 in number, between this & ye Bleech Yard." Below this were the words "el Palmar."

The "River" could only mean Sebastian Creek, not a spot near Cape Kennedy or in the Florida Keys. It meant that the experts had been wrong in locating the sunken fleet.

The "Bleech Yard," the treasure hunters learned, was a flat peninsula near the mouth of the St. Lucie River to the south. Sails were washed in the river, then stretched out to bleach in the sun. "El Palmar" referred to a palm grove belonging to the Ais Indians, whose midden mounds are still visible in the Sebastian area.

Wagner and Kelso pursued their research about the 1715 treasure fleet in the world's richest storehouse of Spanish-American historical documents—the General Archives of the Indies, in Seville, Spain. With the help of its curator, Dr. Don José de la Peña, Wagner obtained a microfilm detailing the background of the late seventeenth- and early eighteenth-century Spanish plate fleets. It told their routes, when and where they sailed, the number of men in the crews, who their captains were, their manifest lists describing the enormous amount of treasure they carried, wreck locations, the amount of salvage recovered, and a description of the salvage campsite—the whole story. But it was all written in archaic Spanish, which neither Wagner nor Kelso could read.

Thus began months of work with language experts in this specialized field of translating, until in the end they had the information they needed.

Fortified with these new clues, Wagner bought a war-surplus metal detector for fifteen dollars and began searching the beaches as he never had before. This time he was seeking the camp that Solórzano had used while his men were salvaging treasure from the fleet. Wagner reasoned that if he could find the camp, it would put him within reach of the treasure galleons.

He followed a copy of Romans' map to what he judged was the approximate campsite and began working the long-handled, platter-sized metal detector over the sand. Within minutes he heard through the detector's earphones a high-pitched whine indicating buried metal—the

TEXT CONTINUED ON PAGE 80

After Kip Wagner had pinpointed the scattered remains of the Spanish treasure fleet that had been wrecked by a hurricane off Florida in 1715, he formed the Real Eight Company to explore them. Among the artifacts that the salvagers recovered were a bottle stopper in the shape of a moth (left), thousands of silver coins like those below, and, opposite, a gold ring (one of more than a dozen found), a round ingot of pure gold weighing more than seven pounds, and an eleven-foot gold chain to which was attached a gold dragon. The dragon is a combination whistle, toothpick, and ear cleaner and was the badge of office of the fleet's commander, General Juan Estéban Ubilla.

rusted springs of a Model-T Ford, as it turned out. Next he unearthed bottle caps, beer cans, bobby pins, the remains of a 1920 coffee grinder. Within a few weeks he had dug up enough worthless trash to set himself up in the junk business. Wagner was disheartened but he searched on, accompanied only by the wheeling gulls and a stray dog.

One day while Wagner was standing on a bluff looking across the undulating green palmetto-scrub that covered the dunes to the west, he noticed a depression in the land that somehow did not fit in with the rest of the scenery. He had felt that his first clue to the Spanish camp would be either a mound or a dish-shaped depression such as this one.

With the dog close at his heels, Wagner plunged through the rough scrub that tore at his clothes. When he finally reached the depression he found a partially filled-in hole containing water. Saltwater springs and holes were common along the ocean front, so it did not impress him. He poked around for a while and decided that what he had sighted was nothing more than a natural dip in the terrain. As he was about to leave, he noticed that the dog was drinking from the water-filled hole.

Fresh water might mean a man-made well, thought Wagner. Maybe this was the campsite after all.

He hurried home for his metal detector. Within an hour he was back, moving the instrument's probe over the sand and listening for the first high-pitched whine. He did not have long to wait. With its first ping, Wagner dropped to his knees and dug. Out of the sand came a ship's spike. Minutes later he uncovered a cannonball. Then the detector broke into a stammering scream. There was metal all over the site and this time it was not tin cans and bobby pins. Wagner felt sure he had found the campsite, but instead of digging up the place, he made a careful survey with his detector and mapped off those areas where it indicated the highest concentration of metal. They covered almost an acre.

Rather than invest in a major excavation that might lead up another blind alley, Wagner wrote to the South Florida Historical Society, explaining what he had found and asking if it could possibly be the old Spanish campsite. After examining the terrain and the artifacts he had found, the society's experts told him they were sure that it was.

Wagner at once began excavating. He cleared the scrub with a rented bulldozer, then settled down to slowly shoveling and sifting his way inch by inch through the sand. Months later he had uncovered hundreds of broken fragments of Mexican and Peruvian pottery, Chinese porcelain, bricks, several musket balls, a bullet mold, a pair of rusty cutlasses lying inches apart as if they had been in a case, three blackened rectangular bricks of silver, and the remains of the kiln that had been used for melting down the salvaged coins into more manageable silver ingots. In the course of the excavation he also found thirteen pieces of eight and the most valuable find of all—a crudely made gold ring with a two-and-one-half-carat diamond surrounded by six tiny diamonds.

By now Wagner had a bad case of treasure fever. On the days he rested from digging at the campsite he swam through the surf, exploring the bottom on a homemade surfboard with a window in it. The reef was fairly close to shore, but for some time he spotted nothing on the bottom that even remotely resembled a shipwreck. Then one day Wagner noted an unfamiliar shape. When he dived to investigate it, he found himself staring at the muzzle of a coral-encrusted cannon. Beside it were four others—all lying in no more than eight or nine feet of water. A short distance away he discovered a huge ship's anchor. Wagner was elated. He knew now why he had been unable to locate the wreck earlier— he had half expected to find a fully rigged galleon on the bottom. Instead, nothing remained of the wooden vessel except its metal fittings, its cannon, and its ballast rocks, all of which could be hidden easily by a few inches of sand. To mark the site of the wreck, Wagner bulldozed a swath through the undergrowth from the campsite to the beach that pointed straight at it.

Kelso, overjoyed at the new find, bought Wagner his first diving rig— an air tank, regulator, flippers, and face mask—to launch his friend properly on his new phase of underwater treasure hunting.

Wagner made a few tentative dives on the wreck, locating several more cannon and a fist-sized clump of blackened silver coins. But it was obvious to him that not only would a proper salvage job take considerable time and money, but it would involve additional manpower and dredging equipment capable of moving large quantities of sand and debris—all of which was presently beyond his reach. Realizing this, Wagner had to be content with making mental notes of the size and distribution of the wreck, and saving the rest for another day.

Shortly afterward he visited another wreck site, whose location was well known to local divers, near Fort Pierce. There he found a handful of scattered coins dating from the 1715 period; but once again, tons of ballast rock, which he could not move alone, thwarted any realistic salvage attempt. He suspected that it would be some time before he could put together the necessary men, machinery, and money, but to insure himself against that day, he obtained a nonexclusive salvage search lease from the state of Florida for a fifty-mile area from Sebastian Inlet to a point north of Stuart, with exclusive pinpoint leases on the wreck sites he had found.

From 1959 to 1960 Wagner gradually gathered the capable, dedicated men he needed. Some were chance acquaintances; others were friends of friends. All were specialists in their fields and no two had the same specialty. But they all shared a severe case of treasure-hunting fever and the determination to wrest a fortune from the sea.

Wagner finally found the boat he needed in the salvage yards at Norfolk, Virginia. It was little more than the hull of a forty-foot dilapidated Navy liberty launch, but it had possibilities. The treasure hunters christened it the *Sampan*. A sand dredge run by a tractor engine was mounted in the bow. A fire hose shot a stream of water through a length of stovepipe to create the suction necessary for vacuuming sand from the bottom. With this and other odds and ends of patched diving equipment, the group launched itself into the treasure salvage business.

Wagner tested his team on the Fort Pierce wreck, knowing that they would not find anything important but feeling that it would be excellent training for the choicer wrecks. Working weekends, the team moved tons of ballast rock to find little more than cannonballs, broken pottery, a copper rim and handle, and a handful of brass nails. Toward the end of the summer diving season the team's spirits had nearly reached their ebb when one of the divers discovered a wedge of solid silver in the Fort Pierce wreck. In no time they recovered three more wedges, which formed a silver "pie" eight inches in diameter. It was estimated that three layers of wedges would have filled a keg weighing one hundred pounds. It was the group's first taste of both hardship and treasure. Wagner felt that the men had earned the right to move on to something bigger.

So, on a bitterly cold morning in January, 1961, they set off for the wreck he had found off the old Spanish campsite. The *Sampan* wallowed through the seething cross currents of Sebastian Inlet and nosed into a fifteen-knot wind. The ominous Atlantic waves looked like elephants' backs. Wagner was apprehensive about the weather, but the others were anxious to go. When they were two and a half miles south of the inlet, they carefully dropped anchor nine hundred feet offshore in a trough between two jagged reefs. Wagner knew that if the boat moved fifty to one hundred feet in either direction, they would share the fate of the galleon they were about to explore.

Harry Cannon and Dan Thompson, the only two divers with wet suits, went over the side to scout the site. A few minutes later one of them surfaced and shouted that he had found several cannon. Wagner hastened to move the boat closer to him. Meanwhile, Dan Thompson, the other diver, had made a discovery of his own. Despite the effort to keep his balance among icy rollers that frequently somersaulted him over the bottom, he had spotted two curious rocklike objects about a foot and a half thick; they had blackish-green sides and were only lightly encrusted in coral. Around them on the white sand lay pieces of eight, singly and in small clusters. But it was the larger objects that claimed Thompson's attention. They were so heavy that he could carry them only some fifty feet toward the *Sampan* before becoming so winded he had to give up. He tried carrying them separately, but after he moved the first lump, he lost sight of the second. In desperation he surfaced for a rope, dived again, and made it fast to one of the lumps.

When Wagner and the others hauled it up, they found that it was a mass of pieces of eight fused together. It weighed seventy-seven pounds and contained from fifteen hundred to two thousand silver coins. The whoops of joy from the *Sampan* could have been heard all the way to Sebastian Inlet.

Then all the divers went over the side into the bone-chilling water whether they were wearing wet suits or not. Minutes later they surfaced clutching handfuls of coins. One of the men had found the large clump of coins that Thompson had lost. Like the first, it contained hundreds of pieces of eight. The divers brought up a steady flow of coins until the early afternoon, when the Atlantic became too rough and they headed for port to celebrate. Altogether they had collected some four thousand silver coins.

Rough seas prevented the treasure hunters from returning to the site for more than a month, and when they did, they were disappointed to find the wreck covered with a thick layer of sand. Once their sand dredge was in operation, however, the coins again began to appear. One diver spent the day sitting on what he thought was a clump of coral while he fanned the sand on the bottom in search of loose coins. When another diver took a closer look at the purplish-black stool, he spotted the edges of coins. It was a solid mass of coins containing two thousand pieces of eight with an estimated value of between thirty thousand and forty thousand dollars!

With that discovery, Wagner and his team of weekend treasure hunters decided to protect their interests by forming a company called Real Eight, after the old Spanish term for pieces of eight. Converting a few of their coins into cash, the group improved some of their equipment and continued harvesting coins.

Despite its success, the salvage operation was not an easy one. The new sand dredge they had bought was so powerful that in minutes it could scoop out a hole in which you could hide a Volkswagen. If the nozzle was not kept buried in the sand all the time, the dredge would pick up the man guiding it and snap him around underwater like the knot on the end of a whip. Even when the weather was good, combers rolling over the reefs created such turbulence that the divers were constantly in danger of being knocked off their feet. These comparatively good conditions lasted only a few weeks during the summer. After that, the Atlantic became so violent that salvage work was out of the question. During the off season, Wagner continued to search the beach with his metal detector, which never failed to lead him to occasional coins. On one of these trips in November he took along his nineteen-year-old nephew, Rex Stocker. Wagner began turning up pieces of eight at the water's edge with his usual regularity, but Stocker, who had no detector, soon grew restless and wandered up near the bluffs above the high-water mark. Suddenly Stocker shouted excitedly and ran toward his uncle with something yellow wrapped around his arm.

Wagner at first thought that the youth had caught a small snake. Then he stared incredulously at what it really was—a tangled, finely wrought gold chain. It had been lying exposed on the sand as if dropped there by a large breaker.

Closer examination at home revealed that it was an exquisitely wrought gold chain eleven feet four and a half inches long with 2,176 individual flower-shaped links. The pendant it supported was a golden dragon about the size of a man's little finger. Part of the dragon's back swiveled out to form a toothpick, and its tail was shaped like a tiny spoon, possibly for cleaning wax out of one's ears. Blowing into the half-opened mouth of the dragon produced a shrill whistle. Various museums appraised the chain and pendant[1] at $40,000 to $60,000. It later sold at a New York auction for $50,000, making it the single most valuable find that Real Eight recovered from the treasure fleet.

The next major discovery occurred in 1963, when the divers operating the sand dredge began turning up hundreds of pieces of broken blue and white porcelain. Digging deeper, they uncovered perfectly preserved cups and bowls neatly stacked exactly as they had been packed almost 250 years before. The treasure fleet's old manifest lists showed that it was K'ang-Hsi porcelain, a variety that was made between 1662 and 1722. Several museums considered the pieces priceless.

Shortly after finding the china, the divers found another long gold necklace bearing a glass-enclosed pendant with traces of miniature oil paintings on each side. Unfortunately, centuries of immersion had all but destroyed the pictures.

As agreed in the salvage leases that Real Eight had obtained from the state, Florida received 25 per cent of all the treasure found. Although the returns had been good, Wagner realized that there were years of salvage work to be done on the Sebastian Inlet site alone, not to mention the seven other wrecks from the 1715 treasure fleet that he had located along the coast. To spread the work and speed the returns, Real Eight took in Mel Fisher and a professional team of treasure hunters from California. Fisher brought with him an electronic instrument that was to revolutionize the Florida operation. It was a magnetometer—a very sensitive underwater metal detector capable of distinguishing between

---

[1] Its age and origin have baffled experts, but it is thought to be Oriental.

ferrous and nonferrous metals. Fisher's team went to work on one of Wagner's wrecks near Vero Beach, recovering about two thousand silver coins in poor condition. The following year they moved to another site south of Fort Pierce and struck gold.

The first several days of diving at the new wreck produced only about one hundred silver coins. Then one of the men, working to the east of the dig, was attracted by a dull gleam in the sand. When he dug it out, he found two solid gold disks, each weighing about seven pounds. A similar disk weighing twenty-two and a half karats sold for $17,500. For several days a storm kept the men from working the site where the disks had been found. When they returned, the water was too murky. On a hunch, Fisher suggested moving even farther east. Seconds after the dredging began, he found a gold doubloon dated 1698. A few days later the group found over two hundred four- and eight-escudo gold coins. Then, with high-pressure excavating equipment, Fisher blasted a fifteen-foot-long, six-foot-wide trench in the bottom and found it carpeted with gold. In one day the divers collected 1,033 doubloons. One of them was a perfectly shaped gold imperial eight-escudo coin about the size of an American silver dollar with the inscription "Phillip V, By the Grace of God, 1714." It is valued today at $10,000.

The estimated value of the gold, silver, jewelry, and artifacts salvaged by Real Eight from the 1715 Spanish plate fleet now exceeds $4 million. A partial list of the major finds reads like the inventory of an imperial treasury, which it was. From the wreck off Fort Pierce, generally believed to be either General Ubilla's store ship *Nuestra Señora de la Regla* or his Dutch *nao*, the salvaged items include fifteen silver wedges averaging less than four pounds each, three clay animals, many cannonballs, and hundreds of broken pieces of K'ang-Hsi china and Mexican pottery. The wreck south of Vero Beach, believed to be de Echeverz's flagship *Nuestra Señora del Carmen y San Antonio*, produced two thousand silver coins, three gold coins, a silver plate, clay pipes, a ship's bell, cannonballs, and fragments of pottery. The wreck south of Sebastian Inlet, believed to be General Ubilla's flagship, yielded hundreds of pounds of loose pieces of eight, twenty clumps of silver coins, including the one weighing seventy-seven pounds, a three-by-two-foot lead-lined wooden chest containing a fused conglomerate of some three thousand silver coins, the golden dragon pendant and chain found on the beach, thirty-six gold coins, two gold rings, a gold-plated sea horse, a gold cross, a part of a gold-plated jewel box, a gold pendant and chain, a silver cross, a silver brooch with miniature oil paintings, fifty pewter plates, twenty silver forks, a silver bottle stopper in the shape of a moth, a silver cup, six silver candlesticks, twenty-eight intact pieces of K'ang-Hsi china, forty-two silver disks eighteen inches in diameter weighing from 44 to 105 pounds, twenty 6-pound silver wedges, many bottles, cannonballs, and muskets. The wreck south of Fort Pierce produced 2,500 silver coins, several thousand gold coins, including a few rare "imperials" valued at $10,000 apiece, four gold chains, sixteen gold rings, three large gold disks averaging seven and a half pounds apiece, one small gold disk that sold for $17,000, two silver disks averaging twenty-seven pounds, six small silver disks and other silver pieces, and an assortment of cannonballs, muskets, and pewter.

No one knows what new treasures remain to be found beneath the sand and shoals that swallowed up the 1715 Spanish plate fleet, but salvage operations are expected to continue for years. Many of the major finds are on permanent exhibit in the Real Eight treasure museum near Cape Kennedy. The others are in bank vaults.

Although millions more may yet be found, nothing will alter the fact that the first silver piece of eight Kip Wagner discovered on the beach near Sebastian Inlet opened a door to history that had been closed for 250 years.

Tired pirates pause for refreshment, as imagined by a nineteenth-century artist.

CHAPTER SIX

Seventeen
Minutes to
Doomsday

*F*une 7, 1692, was oppressively hot
and sultry in Port Royal, Jamaica, a town so wide open to pirates and
privateers that it was called the Treasury of the West Indies—the
World's Wickedest City. The cramped and crowded city of eight thousand was sweltering in a week-long heat wave that some citizens believed
was a prophetic blast straight from hell. When dawn broke that Tuesday
morning, the sea and wind were absolutely motionless, and as the sun
climbed toward its zenith the tepid air grew almost too thick to breathe.
The restless snorting and blowing of hawksbills and loggerheads in the
four turtle crawls on Fishers Row could easily be heard a block away on
Lime Street. Shimmering heat waves danced along the crowded waterfront buildings and quays that lined King's Street. A British merchantman, several Jamaican sloops, and a number of other vessels rode slackly
at anchor at Harbour Side. In the careenage H.M.S. *Swan* lay on her
beam-ends, deserted. The workmen who had been lethargically scrap-
ing her hull had retreated early into the shade of Alderman Beckford's

Wharf for their noonday meal of turtle stew. At the governor's house, Reverend Emmanuel Heath, Rector of St. Paul's, was about to take a glass of wormwood wine with John White, Acting Governor of Jamaica. Several blocks away, a merchant stepped out of a tavern, paused beside a brick wall, and took out his brass pocket watch to see if he had time to reach the cooper's shop before it closed for the noon hour and siesta. Although they did not know it, the merchant and more than two thousand other inhabitants of Port Royal were seventeen minutes away from doomsday.

At 11:40 A.M. three violent earthquakes shook the city. The last and most severe tremor was followed by a huge tidal wave. Within three minutes, the ships in the harbor tore loose from their moorings, walls and buildings collapsed, and nine tenths of the town sank or slid into the sea. One eyewitness who lived through the disaster described what happened: "Betwixt eleven and twelve at noon . . . we felt the house shake and saw the bricks begin to rise in the floor, and at the same instant heard one in the street cry, 'An earthquake!' Immediately we ran out of the house, where we saw all people with lifted up hands begging God's assistance. We continued running up the street whilst on either side of us we saw the houses, some swallowed up, others thrown on heaps; the sand in the streets rise like waves of the sea, lifting up all persons that stood upon it and immediately dropping them into pits; and at the same instant a flood of water breaking in and rolling those poor souls over and over; some catching hold of beams and rafters of houses, others were found in the sand that appeared when the water was drained away, with their arms and legs out. The small piece of ground whereon sixteen or eighteen of us stood (praised be to God) did not sink. As soon as the violent shake was over, every man was desirous to know if any part of his family were left alive. I endeavored to go to my house upon the ruins of the houses that were floating upon the water, but could not. At length I got a canoe and rowed upon the great sea towards my house, where I found several men and women floating upon a wreck out to sea; and as many of them as I could I took into the boat and still rowed on till I came to where I thought my house stood, but could not hear either my wife nor family; so retiring again to that little part of land remaining above water."

"The earth heaved and swelled like the rolling billows," said another account, "and in many places the earth crack'd, open'd and shut, with a motion quick and fast . . . in some of these, people were swallowed up, in others they were caught by the middle, and pressed to death. . . . The whole thing was attended with . . . the noise of falling mountains at a distance, while the sky . . . was turned dull and reddish, like an glowing oven."

Before the sun set that day on Port Royal, more than eighteen hundred buildings had disappeared. All that remained above water was ten acres of dry land in the form of a cay. An incalculable amount of property and wealth was lost. Two thousand perished during the quake, and one thousand survivors died from epidemics that followed it.

Part of the town was rebuilt a few years later, but never again did it enjoy its former prominence. All that remained of the infamous city that sank beneath the sea were the stories and legends that grew up about it in the ensuing centuries. It was said that Port Royal had sunk intact; that the streets had been paved with gold; that a fleet of pirate ships had foundered in the harbor with a cargo of gold and silver bullion beyond man's greatest dreams. As late as 1955, when I was a Florida magazine editor, a well-known deep-sea diver approached me with an article he had written about his exploration of the sunken city. In it he told of walking along underwater avenues flanked by balconies and balustrades of ancient buildings; he told how he had seen the old bell tower of St. Paul's church still standing, its huge coral-encrusted bell swinging in the currents as it perpetually tolled a death knell for Port Royal's lost souls. It made a good story, but we could not use it. Another magazine did, however, and in later years it was this haunting spectacle of St. Paul's tolling bell that was to attract at least one diver-archaeologist to the site of the sunken city.

The first major scientific attempt to investigate the drowned city was made by the Geographic-Smithsonian-Link expedition in the spring of 1959. Edwin Link was the inventor of World War II's famous Link Trainer and many other aeronautical and electronic devices. Sponsored by the National Geographic Society, the Smithsonian Institution, and the Institute of Jamaica, the group arrived aboard Link's newly completed diving and salvage ship, *Sea Diver*—a vessel designed expressly for submarine archaeology. The ninety-one-foot-long steel ship was powered by twin diesel motors and could accommodate twelve people. Two generators supplied electricity for the large compressor that provided air for numerous divers and operated a ten-inch-diameter airlift—a kind of huge vacuum cleaner that sucked up debris for screening as it dredged the bottom. A heavy-duty jetting hose was used for clearing away underwater silt and gravel deposits. A special diving compartment aft could be entered either from the deck or directly from the sea through a large hatch that opened nearly flush with the waterline. Deck booms and electric winches stood ready to hoist cannon or other heavy objects from the sea floor. Thick glass ports in the bow allowed observers to view the bottom in clear water. *Sea Diver* was partially jet-propelled: under her bow on each side of her keel were nozzles through which water could be ejected at high velocity, enabling the vessel to turn in her own length. *Reef Diver*, an eighteen-foot launch on her afterdeck, was propelled entirely by water jet.

The Links had come to Port Royal two years earlier aboard a converted shrimp boat, and their first dive on that trip had destroyed many glittering legends. In twenty to forty feet of water, where the old town had crashed into the sea, all they found was a monotonous mud bottom without the slightest hint of a structure. Hurricanes, tides, and almost three hundred years of silting had completely buried what the earthquake had not destroyed. To make matters worse, the water was always murky from mud carried into the harbor from mountain streams. Using a small, inadequate airlift, they had burrowed four to six feet into the mud before they found any trace of the city—a few cracked brick walls. During their brief stay, they had salvaged one cannon from old Fort James, and then left, intending to return with better equipment.

They had that equipment now, but nothing else had changed in the intervening two years: Port Royal, if anything was left of it, was still a buried city. But this time the Links had a postearthquake map from the British Museum. Used in conjunction with early survey data from the Jamaican government, it showed the locations of the streets and buildings now submerged.

The expedition first set out to scan the sunken city with a portable echo-sounding device they carried aboard the launch. Any abrupt deviation in the bottom profile might indicate the presence of buildings beneath the mud. These were in turn plotted on a chart in relation to existing landmarks. In this way they located and buoyed the fifteen-foot-high walls of Fort James, which their early survey map showed was not far from the king's warehouses. The size of the warehouses and the possibility that they might have contained valuable merchandise under the protection of the Crown persuaded the Links to examine them more closely.

One end of the airlift was attached to a steel barge and the other end was taken to the bottom. A hose from a surface compressor directed a high-pressure stream of air up through the pipe, sucking up silt and debris from the bottom and depositing it onto the deck of the barge for sifting. Divers were to salvage anything they found exposed before the airlift shot it up the tube to the barge.

In the days that followed, the airlift chewed deep holes and trenches in the bottom, but all that appeared in the mud and gravel were bits of pottery and bottles from modern times. The lift was shifted farther out to sea, yet the results were the same.

Apparently the 234-foot-long king's warehouses had been made of wood, and if they contained largely perishable goods such as cotton and tobacco, the divers might search a long time before they stumbled onto anything of value.

Again the search was shifted, this time to a site close to the east wall of Fort James. The airlift had hardly bitten into the bottom when it began sucking up bricks, broken wine bottles, and sections of white clay pipes — all contemporary with old Port Royal. Next came pieces of coal, wall plaster, flint, a variety of bones, roof tiles, and broken dishes.

The most important finds were made at the mouth of the airlift, where the divers brought up first a long-handled brass ladle with a perforated bowl. Then they retrieved pewter spoons, a badly corroded pewter plate, and many fine specimens of greenish-black seventeenth-century glass rum bottles — long-necked containers with flattened, spherical bases — called onion bottles because of their shape. Visibility underwater was about two feet, which meant that divers had to feel their way. The finds were made at the base of a brick wall, and there were more walls. The danger was that the airlift might undermine the walls and cause them to collapse. Other hazards were sea urchins, stingrays, moray eels, and scorpion fish, which lurked, mostly unseen, on the muddy bottom. Sharks and barracudas were sighted nearer the surface, but the divers had no way of knowing, nor were they particularly anxious to know, how close these predators came to them on the bottom.

One morning the airlift was shifted to where the underwater metal detector indicated the presence of hidden metal. Shortly after it bored into the bottom, the divers recovered a large battered copper cooking pot. As Link scooped out the mud from its interior, he found a collection of bleached white bones, some of them still marked by the butcher's cleaver. They were the remnants of a 267-year-old meal—a turtle stew that was never finished.

In the following days it became clear that the expedition was excavating a kitchen. More pots came to light, along with pewter plates and spoons, charred bricks from a fireplace, parts of an iron grill, a grindstone, brass candlesticks, clay pipes, numbers of onion bottles, flat red tiles, and chunks of plaster with a curious twisted pattern on the backs. These finds allowed the Smithsonian experts to piece together an almost exact picture of what the building had looked like before the earthquake. Their map indicated that they were either digging in the Fort James cook house or at Mrs. Littleton's tavern.

Inside the submerged walls of Fort James the metal detector again indicated buried metal. With the jetting hose, the divers uncovered a four-pound cannonball, a lead ball from a swivel gun, and a broken bar shot—two small cannonballs joined by a metal bar designed to cut down rigging and men as it revolved in flight.

While they were exploring walls off the old customs dock, the divers found more onion bottles, one of which was still tightly corked and sealed with a twist of wire. When encrustations were scraped away, liquid was visible in the bottle. A hypodermic needle was inserted through the cork and a small amount of amber liquid drawn out. Link sipped it and grimaced. "Tastes like strongly salted vinegar," he sputtered. "I guess 1692 must have been a bad vintage year."

Close to where the bottle was found, the divers began bringing up dozens of coral-encrusted pieces of metal. When these were hammered open, they were often found to contain nothing more than a black oxydized powder where the object had been. Other chunks, however, revealed recognizable pieces of ship's fittings and tools. Then up came a twenty-foot-long wooden yardarm for a square-rigged sail that looked as though it had never been used. The spar had been spared by the wood-boring worms because it had been completely buried in fine clay.

Another curious find was a wrought-iron swivel gun with a barrel that was heavily banded at close intervals. Mendel Peterson of the Smithsonian Institution identified it as a type made in Spain in the fifteenth century. Even when Columbus first came to America, this kind of gun might have been half a century old, and when Port Royal was destroyed, it was already an antique. What was it doing there and where had it come from?

The gun had been found in an area indicated on the old map as being near Humphrey Freeman's Wharf. The coral-encrusted ship's fittings and tools meant that Freeman might also have owned a ship chandlery. "If this were the case," said Peterson, "perhaps Mr. Freeman was a gun collector and had the unusual piece on display in his shop."

Ed Link suggested an even more intriguing possibility: "It could have come from one of Columbus's ships when he had to strand them in St. Ann's Bay on the north shore."

The expedition might have missed its most important find had not a sharp-eyed diver noticed a flash of metal in the debris shooting from the airlift pipe onto the barge. It was a shiny brass pocket watch with a perforated design on its case. The face was covered with a heavy layer of chalky limestone. Was the watch a relic from the earthquake? Or, for it looked remarkably new, had it been dropped overboard by some careless passenger years later? After carefully cleaning the watch, Link pried open the case. Clearly engraved on the inside of the back was the name of the maker, Paul Blondel. As Link separated the back from the front, a shower of tiny brass wheels and gears fell into his hand. Except for a few particles of dirt, the inside of the watch was surprisingly clean considering its long submersion. Painstakingly he removed the coral encrustation from the face of the watch. The Roman numerals were clearly visible, but the hands had apparently been made of steel like the gear pinions and had disintegrated. The coral deposit he had removed showed the mirror image of the numerals, but again there were no indication of the hands.

In the middle of the seventeenth century Henry Morgan, above, left his native Wales to seek his fortune. Using Port Royal, Jamaica, as his base, he became such a successful pirate that he was knighted by Charles II and appointed lieutenant governor of the island. There Sir Henry died in bed, wealthy and respected, at the age of fifty-three.

By all reports the earthquake had occurred shortly before noon. Link wondered if X-raying the coral disk would reveal something that he could not see with the naked eye. That afternoon he had the X-ray made by a dentist in Kingston, and the next day he had the results. The small negative showed the faint trace of the hands pointing close to the eight and the twelve. He replaced the cake of coral on the face of the watch exactly as it had been when the watch was found.

"It stopped at seventeen minutes of twelve," he said. "Just time enough for the water to have reached the works after the earthquake struck."

Several weeks later Link had proof that the watch had indeed been lost during the disaster. Experts at the Science Museum in London, which houses one of the world's finest collections of old watches, examined the find and said that it had been made by Paul Blondel in Amsterdam in 1686, the last year in which Blondel made watches and six years before Port Royal was engulfed. It looked new when it was found because the case had originally been covered with leather held in place by silver studs that had fitted into the design of perforations on the case. Apparently the leather had been stripped off as the watch rode up the airlift, leaving the bright, shiny artifact that had caught the diver's eye.

After ten weeks of work on the sunken city, the approaching hurricane season made it necessary for the expedition to cease operations and return to Florida. Despite what they had accomplished, the Links realized that they had only scratched the surface of the city that still lay buried beneath the sea.

Port Royal, Jamaica, was much reduced after the earthquake, as this view shows.

CHAPTER SEVEN

Salvaging the City Beneath the Sea

$\mathcal{S}$ix years elapsed before anything more was done at Port Royal. Then, in 1965, the Jamaican government hired Robert Marx to make a large-scale excavation of the sunken city. Since he had found and lost the *Monitor,* Marx had left the Marines and studied to become a specialist in marine archaeology. After that he investigated ancient wrecks near Bermuda, took part in the recovery of two hundred thousand artifacts from a Spanish galleon that had sunk in 1741 off Quintana Roo, Mexico, and probed Mayan ruins in the jungles of Yucatán. When his historical research took him to Spanish archives, he dived to explore sunken Roman cities and shipwrecks off the Iberian peninsula. In 1962 he sailed from Spain as co-organizer and navigator aboard a replica of Columbus' *Niña,* which left Palos, Spain, and arrived in San Salvador, Bahama Islands, to duplicate the explorer's voyage of 1492.

As a marine archaeologist, Marx welcomed the opportunity to excavate Port Royal with the same enthusiasm that his counterparts must have felt when they uncovered Pompeii two centuries earlier.

Marx's main desire was to explore the sunken city scientifically, according to the established principles of archaeology. But once he familiarized himself with the site, he realized that a proper investigation would take years; indeed, that it would be the largest marine excavation project ever attempted. Moreover, he was faced with two major handicaps. The first was a severe shortage of funds; the second, insufficient time. There were plans to turn modern Port Royal into a tourist attraction and to dredge a deep-water port, which would permanently destroy over half the sunken city. Since Marx had no control over this decision, it was with a certain amount of urgency that he began to resurrect old Port Royal's past.

During an inspection dive on a clear December day in 1965, Marx found that visibility was less than an arm's length. Artifacts were scattered haphazardly over the ocean floor. When a large freighter dropped its anchor near Marx and dragged it across the bottom, it gouged a trench four feet wide, five feet deep, and two hundred feet long. Marx found that the anchor, instead of revealing artifacts, had unearthed large numbers of Coca-Cola bottles, hub caps, tin cans, and other modern debris. Quite obviously the depth that an object was buried was not going to be an indication of its age. Nevertheless, Marx intended to excavate in layers, keeping an accurate record of the level at which each artifact was found. The Jamaican government provided him with a gridded chart of old Port Royal, and he set out mapping a 200-by-300-foot section of the city that had contained the jails, fish and meat markets, craftsmen's shops, and private houses. Since there were no funds to hire assistants, he tackled the job himself, using a metal detector to locate concentrations of metal, and an eight-foot-long metal probe to locate walls buried under the mud. Good weather enabled Marx to dive twelve hours a day, but even so the job took months. By the time he had completed it, he had the funds to assemble a diving team and to buy some much-needed equipment.

His new assistants were Wayne Roosevelt and Kenute Kelly, an amateur swimming champion and a professional salvage diver. The new equipment was a recently invented hookah rig—a floating air compressor that pumped air through two hoses to the divers below. As long as the compressor engine was refueled, the divers could work all day

By moonlight, a boatload of pirates swarm aboard a ship that is anchored for the night.

on the bottom without being encumbered by scuba tanks. To vacuum away silt and debris, Marx built an airlift with a four-inch-diameter tube. It was smaller than those normally used, and a screen over its mouth prevented objects from being sucked up before the diver could rescue them. An even finer screen on the barge that caught the outpourings of the airlift strained out objects as small as pins and beads. A crew of four manned the barge.

Long before Marx finished mapping his first quadrant, he realized that Port Royal would not be another Pompeii. The Roman city had been buried for almost two thousand years, yet almost everything had remained exactly as it was the day it was covered quickly with volcanic ash. Archaeologists had found fully furnished buildings intact, the final moments of their occupants preserved in solidified ash. Port Royal was less than three hundred years old, but the calamity that had overwhelmed it had been so violently destructive that there was little hope of finding anything intact. Buildings had been shattered, belongings scattered, and what the quake had failed to destroy, the sea had done its best to obliterate. But the archaeologist and his small crew persisted.

On May 1, 1966, the group was working a spot about 120 feet from shore. Barely a foot under the mud one artifact after another turned up. By the end of the first hour the excavators had filled three baskets with clay smoking pipes, ceramic shards, unbroken onion bottles, and various coral-encrusted iron objects. It was a good start. Then Marx found a fallen brick wall and wondered if anything of value had been caught under it. Since it was unlikely that early salvagers had bothered lifting walls, he attacked it with the airlift. As the powerful suction ate a trench along one side, pewter spoons, a meat platter, and stacked plates began tumbling into the hole. Despite his excitement, Marx noted that the wall was slowly tilting. He backed off, regrouped his forces, and debated whether or not to dismantle the wall brick by brick from the top. At that moment, Kelly shot forward and disappeared into the trench undermining the wall. Marx was about to go after him when he came out jubilantly clutching a pewter tankard and plate.

Marx was elated with the finds but he wanted no injuries, and he signaled the divers to stay clear of the wall until he had leveled it. Swimming around to the opposite side, he began to dig. Seconds later he recovered a cluster of four pewter spoons. Recklessly, Marx dug deeper than he intended. The next thing he knew a heavy weight slammed him into the mud. The wall had toppled over, pinning his head and torso to the bottom. It had smashed the airlift pipe but fortunately it had not broken his air hose. Instantly the barge crew knew that something was wrong. Kelly dived to investigate, missing Marx at first because visibility was less than a foot. When he found him, he disconnected the airlift and used its air hose to jet away the sediment under Marx's trapped body. It was not the safest maneuver, but it was certainly the most logical one at the time. There was a good chance that loosening the debris under Marx would cause the wall to settle further, trapping Kelly as well. Fortunately, however, the wall held. From then on, Marx made a standing rule: Take a wall apart before it takes you apart. Even so, Port Royal's unstable walls proved to be a constant hazard.

Not long afterward Marx was confronted with a puzzle. In the center of the sunken city he began to find numerous artifacts from a ship—nails, caulking tools, draft markers, brass fittings. The brass and copper artifacts were stamped with the English "broad arrow," which meant they had come from a ship rather than from a ship supply shop. But where was the wreck? Even if all the ship's timbers had been destroyed by woodboring worms, there should have been a huge pile of ballast rock left to mark the spot. Yet there was none. He was baffled.

A week later Marx found the keel and ribs of a 250-to-300-ton ship. Brick walls above and below the keel dated her as a victim of the quake. Scattered cannon nearby and the lack of artifacts normally found on merchant ships indicated that she was a warship. Marx initiated a lengthy correspondence with the British Admiralty and searched old records in an attempt to learn which British ship had been lost at Port Royal during the earthquake.

He discovered that H.M.S. *Swan,* a 74-foot-long, 305-ton warship, was reported to have disappeared during the disaster. Most important of all, Marx learned that her ballast had been removed so that she could be tilted on her beam-ends in the careening area on shore to have her hull scraped and repaired. He reasoned that without her one hundred tons of ballast, the ship would have been light enough so that the tidal wave could have carried her from the careenage to the middle of the old town where he had discovered the wreck. Marx was certain that he had found the *Swan*.

Limited visibility in the murky waters of Port Royal Harbor caused unexpected accidents. Airlift operators cut their hands on broken glass and were pricked by sea urchins. The sides of excavations caved in on divers before they could see the impending danger. One day Marx's most proficient diver, Kelly, was surfacing through the gloom when something bumped him. As he turned, a manta ray measuring twelve feet between its wing tips embraced him. Mantas are not normally dangerous, but under certain circumstances their great weight could crush a man. Prudently, Kelly remained perfectly still until the playful manta unfolded its wings and released him.

On another occasion Marx was nudged from behind. Without turning from his work, he reached back to push away the intruder. His hand touched something rougher than sandpaper. Marx spun around and found himself staring at a large hammerhead shark. Happily, the shark was as surprised as the diver and swam swiftly away.

Not all sharks were so easily frightened. One morning an eight-and-a-half-foot hammerhead bumped the divers repeatedly. Twice its fins fouled Marx's air hose, ripping it off. The obnoxious visitor was making a nuisance of itself, but rather than kill it and risk having its blood attract others, Marx posted a guard and continued working. But the shark had made one pass too many at Kelly. Unknown to Marx, he swam for the barge and his speargun.

While Marx labored below, the barge crew was coaxing the shark closer so that Kelly could make a quick kill. If the shark were only wounded, no one would be safe in the water. As the hammerhead glided past, Kelly sighted and fired. The spear thudded into the shark's brain, and the crew quickly hauled the writhing monster into the skiff before its blood could spread.

Despite these dangers, Marx and his men were recovering some remarkable artifacts. Since early seamen were in the habit of leaving their clay pipes at every tavern they visited, the excavators found hundreds of them. On one occasion they even recovered a complete leaf of tobacco that was none the worse for its long submersion at the bottom of the sea. A wooden chest containing twenty-one small glass medicine bottles marked the location of an apothecary's shop; pieces of leather, awls, nails, heels, and shoes were salvaged where a cobbler's shop once stood; and more ship's fittings, this time unmarked, were unearthed from a ship chandler's shop. Bones stacked three feet deep were found in an area forty feet long and fifteen feet wide. In one section there were fish bones; in another, the bones of cattle, pigs, and horses. Marx had found the city's fish and meat markets. Shortly afterward he was confronted with another puzzling find. Turtle was the staple meat at old Port Royal. The hawksbills and loggerheads were confined alive in four wood-fenced enclosures called turtle crawls. When the excavators began sifting the silt from these areas they were surprised to find the fence posts still standing and the pens filled with thousands of turtle bones. Why had the turtles not escaped when the tidal wave swept over the crawls? The only explanations Marx could offer was either that the turtles had been suffocated by an avalanche of mud, or that their flippers had been bound together—a common practice of the day.

One of the most exciting moments of the dig was when Marx discovered two standing buildings. Both were buried and required painstaking excavation with the airlift. He removed mud from around the exterior walls of the first building and had just begun digging out the interior when lack of light forced him to quit for the day. The next morning he was disappointed to find that the walls had fallen during the night. He approached the second building differently. Each time he removed a foot of silt from the interior, he did the same around the exterior so that pressures inside and outside the structure were always equal. It took a full day to remove a five-foot depth of mud and reveal a building thirty-four feet long and seventeen feet wide, with walls two feet thick. The next morning the divers were pleased to find that the walls were still standing. But that was the only pleasant occurrence of the day. First the compressor on their hookah rig refused to pump any more air and the divers were forced to switch to scuba. A few minutes later Kelly cut his hand on broken glass and had to be sent to the doctor. Roosevelt and Marx continued working until the building was almost completely excavated. Then Roosevelt developed a sinus headache and Marx sent him to the surface. Since no one was to dive alone (for safety reasons), that ended the day's work. However, Marx feared that the walls might collapse during the night and remained behind to complete a sketch of the building. As he approached to examine the entrance, a wall collapsed, knocking him out and pinning him to the floor of the harbor. When he awoke, his mask was gone and his eyes were smarting from dirt and salt water. He had been prevented from drowning only because he had fallen forward and the wall's weight had pressed his face against the purge button of his mouthpiece regulator, giving him all the air he needed while unconscious. He did not know how long he had been out or how much air remained in his tank. But one fact was clear: there was no one to rescue him.

He tried to push the wall off his back but it would not yield. All he could do was dig straight ahead with his hands. After what seemed like ages, his fingertips found the edge of the wall. Hunching and wiggling his body from side to side, he finally crawled far enough through his man-made tunnel to free his head and arms. Then his regulator caught between two bricks and stopped him.

He tried to back up, to turn sideways, but he was stuck. His air supply was dwindling rapidly; it was becoming more difficult to breathe. Mustering all his strength, he jerked forward. The regulator broke. Another heave and his shoulders and chest were free. With a final push he was clear of the wall and kicking for the surface.

Despite the accidents, Marx's luck was unbelievably good. There seemed no end to the artifacts, and he was accumulating one of the largest hoards of pewter ever found. Then he recovered what he felt was the single most important find of the entire excavation. It was a round object thickly encrusted with coral, and his metal detector indicated the presence of nonferrous metal inside. An X-ray outlined a man's pocket watch. Careful removal of the limestone revealed a watch similar to that found by the Link expedition, except that this one was made of silver and was remarkably well preserved, even to the Roman numerals and the name of the maker — Gibbs of London — inscribed on its face.

Almost immediately after this discovery days passed when the divers returned empty-handed. Marx chafed, for he was already racing against the moment when the dredge was to begin on the deep-water harbor. His wife suggested that he try another site, but Marx felt certain that by following the original plan and enlarging the hole they were currently working on, more artifacts were bound to appear. None did, however, and his crew grew gloomy. Finally, in desperation, Marx handed his wife a chart of the site and asked her to pick a spot. She pointed to an area about a hundred feet north of the hole, and the next day he moved his operations there.

In the first few hours it seemed as if the jinx had followed them. Nothing turned up. Marx was excavating around a coral head when he had to leave the dig to make an urgent telephone call. Minutes later one of the barge crew ran after him with the news that Kelly had found four Spanish pieces of eight in almost perfect condition. Silver exposed for a long time to salt water usually turns black. But except for a slight tarnish, these coins looked newly minted.

And there were hundreds more coins, each in the same splendid condition. Marx discovered why when he found the remains of a wooden chest that had protected the silver for centuries.

By the time word of the find had leaked out, the treasure's value was so magnified that the excavators were forced to cease work for several weeks while police cleared the area of curious people.

Marx took advantage of the lull to do some research, for the coins were Spanish, minted in Lima, Peru. The keyhole plate from the old chest bore the coat of arms of the king of Spain, and knowing Port Royal's infamous history, Marx suspected that the treasure was plunder from one of the Spanish fleets. Then he learned that in 1690—two years before the quake—three Spanish treasure galleons had been wrecked near Jamaica. Since Port Royal's inhabitants had recovered a considerable amount of the cargo, he decided that this was probably where the chest of coins had come from.

In the following months Marx and his men surfaced with an enormous number of artifacts. A cook house yielded hundreds of dinner plates, silverware, bottles, pots and pans. From under fallen brick walls they retrieved many priceless plates, bowls, tankards, porringers, and other artifacts made of pewter and silver, as well as complete ceramic mugs, cups, bowls, plates, candlesticks, pots, skimmers, ladles, buttons, buckles, and many items of iron, brass, copper, lead, glass, wood, bone, and leather. They amassed six tons of bones, most of them from turtles in the market area. They also found several hundred human bones, probably those of victims trapped by falling walls during the disaster. The majority of the finds dating from the 1692 earthquake were found from four to nine feet below the harbor floor, but the divers usually continued to excavate to a depth of twelve feet. On several occasions they found artifacts that predated the quake and indeed the pirate town. These were Arawak Indian pottery fragments, fishing sinkers, ax heads, a stone metate for grinding corn, a projectile point, and a mold of unknown use, indicating that in earlier times Port Royal had been an Indian settlement.

In May, 1967, Marx suffered his worse accident. He was at the bottom of a deep trench that he and Kelly were excavating when a coral head twelve feet in diameter and weighing at least a ton crashed down on him. Fortunately, most of its weight was supported by piles of loose bricks Marx had stacked on both sides of him. Still, he was pinned down, unable to move. Kelly worked for an hour but could not budge the block. Then he surfaced to get help. Although neither of the two men on the barge had ever used scuba equipment before, Kelly wasted no time getting them rigged and down to the bottom. The three of them finally rolled the huge coral head aside, and Marx emerged. He had slipped a disk in his back while arching his body in an attempt to help, and it put him out of action for several weeks.

In July Marx found several thousand more Spanish silver coins, a large amount of silverware, gold rings, cuff links, and most remarkable of all, a fourteen-inch-high porcelain figurine of a woman holding a child on her lap. Research proved it to be a statue of Kuan Yin, the Goddess of Mercy of Chinese Buddhists. Since Kuan Yin has been worshiped for over nine hundred years, the presence of the Chinese statue at old Port Royal supported the belief that sometime in its history the ancient city had been a major hub of waterborne trade.

The discovery of the new treasure subjected the archaeological team to a more serious problem than curious tourists. When the criminal element of Port Royal learned of their find, they threatened to cut themselves in for a share. Not only did the police have to guard the diggers against intrusions by the public, but now they had to protect their lives as well. To further complicate matters, the treasure became a political issue. One faction claimed that the find was larger than had been reported in the newspapers and that the Jamaican government was using the balance for illegal purposes. Further excavation was halted until the Jamaican Parliament resolved the dispute. When work resumed, Marx hoped that he would not soon find another treasure.

The excavation continued successfully until the end of May, 1968, when Marx called a halt to the operation. In two and a half years, he had collected an enormous number of artifacts that were badly in need of preserving and cataloging—jobs that would keep a team of specialists busy for years. Meanwhile, the Jamaican government had announced that the proposed harbor dredging would not take place after all.

Port Royal, the infamous city that sank beneath the sea, may prove to be the most important marine archaeological site in the western hemisphere, for Marx estimated that his team recovered less than 5 per cent of what is there.

William Phips was knighted for salvaging the enormously rich Hispaniola treasure.

CHAPTER EIGHT

The Saga of Silver Shoals

More than half a century before the ill-fated Spanish treasure fleet of 1715 was scattered across the Florida reefs by a hurricane, the misfortunes of a similar armada were responsible for making an American sea captain an English knight and eventually the governor of Massachusetts.

On September 13, 1659, a *Flota* of thirty treasure-laden ships set sail from Havana for Spain. One of the flagships of the fleet was *Nuestra Señora de la Concepción*, whose admiral was forced to sail against his better judgment. Before leaving Havana, he had complained that his galleon not only was unseaworthy but was heavily overloaded with treasure. The ship's hull was rotten and had not been repaired since the admiral had set sail from Spain the year before. But it was the hurricane season and the treasure fleet could delay no longer.

The galleons had been at sea for only a day and a half when *Nuestra Señora* began leaking so badly that the commanding general ordered the vessels back to Havana for repairs. Divers immediately patched

Nuestra Señora's rotten timbers, and twenty-four hours later the silver fleet again put to sea. This time it got as far as the narrowest part of the straits between Florida and the Bahama Islands. There it was struck by a severe hurricane. *Nuestra Señora*'s ancient timbers were wrenched apart by the violent seas, and she began to take water. Her sails were shredded by the howling winds, and the crew was forced to chop down her masts to prevent the ship from foundering. By morning, when the storm's fury abated, the galleon—miraculously still afloat—had become separated from the other ships in the fleet. With her pumps working day and night, temporary sails were rigged and she tried to limp toward Puerto Rico for repairs. But the storm had blown the galleon far off course, and a week later the crew awakened in the middle of the night to find that they were surrounded by foam-flecked reefs. When the anchors were dropped, the hawsers snapped one by one as the seas drove the disabled vessel closer to the rocks. Longboats were launched in an attempt to pull the galleon through a narrow channel between the shoals. All day the crew rowed, but the tide swept the galleon against first one coral head, then another. By nightfall she had gained only a few hundred yards. Several of the galleon's twenty bronze cannon were then put over the side as anchors to hold the ship fast until daylight. But during the night a wind sprang up, causing the vessel to strain against her moorings until the ropes parted. The wind caught the galleon's high-pitched stern and drove her swiftly toward the treacherous reefs. With a grinding crash she ripped open her hull on one reef and swung over to ground on another. And there she stayed, caught in the valley between two reefs, her prow sinking into eight fathoms of water while her stern rose into the air at a crazy angle. The survivors huddled on the exposed portion of the wreck until morning, when they fashioned rafts from whatever was salvageable. These they dangerously overloaded with chests of silver and plate that had been stored in the admiral's quarters. Then the castaways headed south in a direction they hoped would bring them to land.

Unfortunately, no one knew exactly where they were. The ship's pilots insisted that they had been on the Anegada reefs between Puerto Rico and Hispaniola when they had foundered. The admiral disagreed. He felt certain that they were still north of Hispaniola, on the Ambrosian

Banks. As it turned out, he was correct. The few rafts that made shore landed at various points along the north coast of Hispaniola (the West Indies island that today is divided between Haiti and the Dominican Republic). Of the 514 people aboard *Nuestra Señora* when she struck the reef, only 190 survived.

Strangely enough, Spain did not undertake salvage operations. This was perhaps because Spanish shipping at that time was under continual harassment by pirates and privateers, many of whom were sent out from France and England specifically for that purpose. In such cases it was not uncommon for the admirals of stranded galleons to burn their ships to the waterline so there would be less chance of their valuable cargoes being discovered and salvaged by ships of other nations.

In the years that followed the sinking of the treasure galleon, however, many attempts were made by others to find it. Yet the exact location of the wreck remained a mystery. There was uncertainty even among the old sailors of the West Indies who claimed to have firsthand information about the wreck. To the southwest of the Turks Islands lay what the English called Handkerchief Shoal and the Abroxes. Was this where the galleon sank? To the southeast of the Abroxes lay the Ambrosian Banks and the "North Riff." Perhaps that was the place. Directly south of the Ambrosian Banks about midway to Hispaniola lay an oval reef known as the South Riff. That too was a possibility. Ships of all nations searched these waters for the valuable wreck, but despite all efforts *Nuestra Señora* might as well have vanished from the face of the earth.

On April 13, 1683, twenty-four years after the galleon had disappeared, King Charles II of England commissioned two vessels, the frigate *Faulcon*, under Captain George Churchill, and the sloop *Bonetta*, under Captain Edward Stanley, to find and salvage *Nuestra Señora's* treasure. They searched unsuccessfully for three years before returning to England. Their only clue was the tale of one Thomas Smith, a seaman who claimed to have seen the Spanish wreck on the Ambrosian Banks. According to Smith, the galleon was located near a rock that rose nearly fifty feet from the ocean. The hull lay about forty feet away, wedged between reefs that were "heaped high with sows and pigs [large and small molded blocks] of silver." Smith explained that his captain had not tried to salvage the treasure because a storm had come up and the ship had had to leave before it was washed onto the reefs.

Meanwhile, the man who was to solve the riddle of the lost galleon was sailing in another part of the world. He was William Phips, an American farm boy born in Maine in 1650. He was a big, strong, fearless, kindhearted man until he was upset. Then, it was said, he was a holy terror with boots, fists, sword, or pistols.

Phips had always been particularly fascinated by the tales about pirates' treasure he heard along the American coast. He went to sea first as a ship's carpenter and later as the master of his own ship. Wherever he sailed he collected all the information he could about rich wrecks and buried treasure troves. Gradually he accumulated maps and charts supposedly giving the location of these lost riches. From sailors he met in his travels he acquired a small treasure of his own—several coral-encrusted pieces of eight, some silver and gold trinkets, and a few bejeweled weapons. Armed with these modest riches, Phips sailed to England, where he requested an audience with King Charles II. The good sea captain apparently convinced the king that he alone knew the whereabouts of the Hispaniola treasure, for King Charles lent him a small naval ship, the *Rose Algier,* and commissioned him to salvage the treasure.

The *Rose Algier* carried a crew of ninety seamen who were, as the salty phrase of the day went, "the rakings and scrapings of hell." But troublemakers soon learned that despite their captain's outward good nature, he knew how to use his maul-like fists and big sea boots. On one occasion when the crew threatened mutiny in the waist of the ship, Captain Phips coolly surveyed the situation from behind the muzzle of a swivel gun mounted on the poop deck and told the mutineers that it was loaded with pistol balls, "one for each of you." The mutinous crew retired to reconsider.

For almost two years Phips vainly scoured the Ambrosian Banks and the waters north of Hispaniola. His crew threatened to mutiny a second time and tried to persuade him to turn pirate with the *Rose Algier.* But once again Phips outwitted them. After that he sailed for Jamaica and hired new hands to continue his search.

This time he sailed to Puerto Plata, a port on the northern coast of

Hispaniola nearest the banks where the wreck was said to be. There he met a survivor of the shipwrecked galleon who gave him information that he was certain would lead him to the wreck. But he searched the Ambrosian Banks again without success. Finally, when his supplies ran low, he was forced to return to England empty-handed.

While he had been away, his benefactor, King Charles II, had died and been replaced by King James II, who promptly had Captain Phips thrown into jail for obtaining a naval ship, as he said, "under false pretenses."

When Phips was released three months later he went to see the Duke of Albermarle and once again demonstrated his remarkable persuasive abilities. Not only did the bluff captain succeed in capturing the interest and financial support of the duke and several of his wealthy friends, but he obtained two ships from them — the *James and Mary* and the *Henry of London* — with which to carry on his search for the Hispaniola treasure. His backers secured a royal patent granting them exclusive rights to the wrecks, providing the king received a tenth of whatever was found.

Phips returned to the West Indies as commander of the *James and Mary*, a two-hundred-ton ship carrying twenty-two cannon. Accompanying him was the ten-ton frigate the *Henry of London* with fifty guns, commanded by Francis Rogers, Phips's trusted second mate aboard the *Rose Algier*. The two ships were equipped with the latest salvaging equipment of the day.

At Puerto Plata Phips spent nearly a month taking on supplies, preparing his equipment, and trading with the inhabitants. Finally, on January 13, 1687, he sent the *Henry* to search for the wreck some twenty leagues to the north. Almost a month later the frigate returned and Rogers told Phips a long, sorrowful tale of failure. But even as he spoke, Rogers slipped a large oblong bar of silver out from under the table where they sat.

In reply to Phips's barrage of excited questions, Rogers explained what had happened. After fruitlessly searching the north side of the Ambrosian Banks, the *Henry* had moved to the south side and anchored about a mile and a half from the shoals in the latitude 20° 37' north. From that point Rogers and a diver went out in a small boat, and another crew with two divers used a *periagua* — a cottonwood canoe capable of carrying eight to ten oarsmen for working close to the reefs. For days they searched the surf breaking on the shoals, each night returning to the ship, which was moored a safe distance away in deep water. Late in the last day of their discouraging search, one of the divers spotted an unusually beautiful sea feather growing on the bottom. Thinking that it would make an interesting curio, he went overboard to retrieve it. Seconds later he surfaced and excitedly told the others that there were several large cannon lying near the sea feather. Hardly daring to believe that they had at last stumbled onto the wreck, the diver went down again. This time he returned with a "sow," one of the oblong bars of silver with which Rogers had surprised Phips. Before marking the spot with a buoy and returning to the ship for the night, Rogers' divers recovered "two sows, 51 pieces of eight, a bar and a champeen and some broken plate." They worked the wreck for the next three days, finding more "sows and dowboys of silver" and nearly three thousand pieces of eight. Then the weather turned bad, the seas became treacherous, and the *Henry* returned to Puerto Plata.

The reason the wreck had not been discovered earlier was that it had become completely overgrown with coral. As Thomas Smith, the seaman who claimed to have seen it, had said, the wreck rested between two rocks in six to eight fathoms of water. Other searchers could have passed, and probably did pass, within an oar's length of it without realizing how close they were to making their fortune. Once shipworms disfigure a ship's recognizable features, and the sea layers the remnants with a patina of coral, there is little left to identify its original form. In this case, however, Rogers' diver recognized the ship's cannon, although they too were partially hidden beneath a young growth of coral.

Captain Phips stocked the *Henry* and the *James and Mary* with enough supplies for an extended stay at sea; then both ships sailed to the wreck site.

Phips's ships anchored a mile from the reef, and longboats took the salvagers to the wreck. Sailors with long-handled rakes began fishing up bars and plate of silver bullion while four divers descended six to eight fathoms into the heart of the galleon to recover bags and chests of coins. Phips had a diving tub which could be lowered to the bottom so that its imprisoned chamber of air would give the divers additional working time underwater, but he was unable to use it because the wreck lay at a sharp angle. Every day except Sunday Phips's men worked for nearly two months salvaging the treasure, which was carefully recorded and stored aboard the *James and Mary.*

Hardly a week after they had started, the ships were joined by two smaller vessels from Bermuda and Jamaica. Phips knew both of the captains from his earlier treasure-hunting ventures, so he agreed to let them join the salvage operations on shares in exchange for the use of their boats and divers. A few weeks later one of the visiting boats damaged a rudder on the reefs and was forced to sail to Jamaica for repairs. Before leaving, the captain promised to tell no one of the treasure and to return to the site as quickly as possible. When he did not reappear at the expected time, Phips began to worry. He was afraid the damaged vessel might have been captured by French pirates who freely roamed the West Indies. If this had happened, he reasoned, the pirates would soon descend like vultures, taking everything he had found.

To make matters worse, the daily routine of handling a fortune in gold and silver was beginning to tell on Phips's men. They knew that enough treasure was stored in the hold of the *James and Mary* to make each of them wealthy for life. They spoke openly of taking over the ships and forcing the captains to sail for a port that offered refuge to pirates. Phips waited until their threats grew serious. Then he mustered the mutinous men on deck and told them that at that very moment an officer was below with a lighted fuse ready to touch off a powder train that led to the magazine. He said that he had nothing to lose anyway, because if he returned to England without the treasure, he would surely be hanged. On the other hand, if they would behave themselves and continue their work, he would see to it that everyone received a fair share of the treasure once it arrived safely in England. Satisfied with this arrangement, the men went back to work.

Although he had handled this dangerous situation tactfully, Phips grew progressively more worried about what he would do if pirates attacked.

Finally he decided he could wait no longer. He would sail his two ships to the Turks Islands, leaving the Bahamian vessel behind to work the wreck for an additional week. If the Jamaican sloop had not re-

TEXT CONTINUED ON PAGE 120

Sir Peter Lely painted this portrait of Charles II, the British monarch who equipped the persuasive American farm boy William Phips for his first Caribbean treasure hunt.

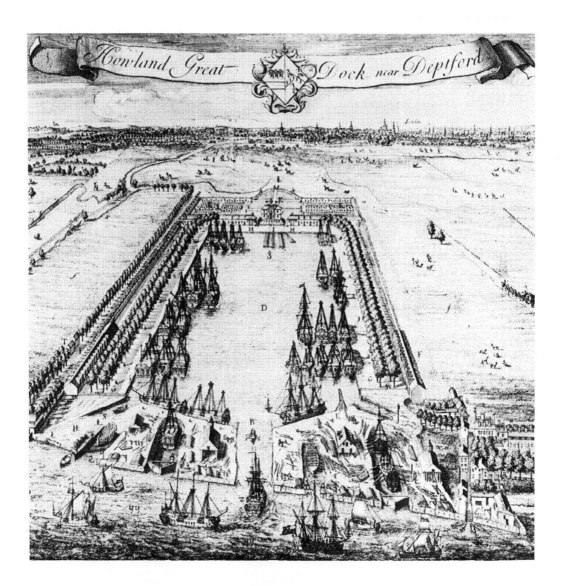

William Phips's first treasure-hunting ship, the Rose Algier, *might well have been built in the royal shipyard at Deptford (above). At left are the two sides of the medal struck to commemorate Phips's successful second attempt to find the Hispaniola hoard.*

turned by then, the Bahamian boat was to join Phips at the Turks Islands.

A little over a week later the Bahamian vessel arrived with no news of the missing sloop, but with more than a ton of silver that had been recovered from the wreck in those few days. Phips paid the captain and crew of the Bahamian sloop their share, and then the two British ships set sail for England, where Phips received a hero's welcome.

According to Admiralty records, the treasure consisted of 37,538 pounds of pieces of eight; 27,556 pounds 4 ounces of silver bars and cakes; 374 pounds of silver plate; 25 pounds 7 ounces of gold, and a miscellaneous collection of less valuable jewels and trinkets. True to his word, Phips set aside 3,070 pounds 3 ounces of the treasure as his crew's share. The total value of the treasure is generally believed to have amounted to between one million and two million dollars. The Crown received its one tenth, and the remainder was distributed according to the agreement Phips had reached with the Duke of Albemarle and the other backers. As an additional reward, Phips was knighted and given a royal commission to return to America as High Sheriff of Massachusetts colony. Later he became its governor.

Once the clamor over his astonishing feat subsided, Phips's backers wanted to know why he had stopped salvage operations when there was obviously considerably more treasure to be recovered. He explained the circumstances surrounding his hasty departure. Now that word of his discovery was out, he urged that a full-scale salvage fleet be dispatched at once before the rest of the treasure was scavenged by others.

This time he had no trouble enlisting support. Five months later three ships were outfitted with trustworthy crews and divers. Two were heavily armed for the protection of the third, which carried the chains, grapnels, powder, nets, baskets, dredges, and diving tubs. Never before had England seen such a well-equipped treasure-hunting expedition.

When Phips reached the Ambrosian Banks, he was appalled to see a score of vessels already working the wreck. Seeing the British, many of the others hastily departed, apparently fearing confiscation of their valuable cargoes. Those that remained agreed to work with Phips in return for shares in whatever was found.

But this time the operation was a disappointment. Phips had salvaged most of the easily accessible treasure on his last trip. Since then, hundreds of other treasure hunters had raised as much or more bullion as Phips had. Now the pickings were so sparse that after a few days even the vessels that had chosen to stay and work on shares quietly left.

Undaunted, Phips felt certain that all previous salvage efforts had merely skimmed the surface of the greater treasure which lay concealed in the heavily coral-encrusted forward section of the wreck.

The divers, working with pikes, could break off only small fragments of coral. Grapnel hooks dragged from above were equally ineffectual against the thick limestone shield. Phips attached an iron bar to the end of a forty-foot spar, fitted it to the prow of a longboat, and repeatedly rammed it into the unyielding barrier. For a month Phips hammered vainly at the coral by one means and another. Finally he had his divers place a waterproofed keg of powder in the coral directly over the treasure room. Next, he inserted a fuse into a long bamboo cane and had his divers attach it to the keg of explosives. Then Phips ignited the fuse on the surface and waited. The experiment failed when the burning fuse split the cane, letting in water that dampened the powder.

A second experiment with underwater explosives was no more successful, and finally the expedition returned to England with only a few pieces of broken silver plate. Sir William Phips never revisited the site of his greatest triumph. Instead he returned to his wife in Massachusetts, went on to become a respected governor of that growing colony, and eventually returned to London, where he died on February 18, 1695.

Phips's feat in recovering part of the Hispaniola treasure became one of the milestones of treasure hunting. Ever since, ships from both continents have searched the treacherous, remote forty-mile-stretch of reefs that came to be known as the Silver Shoals, hoping to find the treasure Phips had missed. One of the most recent and most publicized ventures was the elegantly equipped team of scientists, archaeologists, and underwater specialists of the French oceanographic research ship, the *Calypso,* commanded by Jacques-Yves Cousteau. Although they found and excavated a coral-encased wreck, it proved to be of much later origin than *Nuestra Señora de la Concepción.* Fantastic legends have grown up about the plate fleet lost on Silver Shoals, but to this day there is no record of anyone having rediscovered Phips's Spanish galleon.

This portrait of Theodosia Burr Alston was found aboard a derelict at Nag's Head.

CHAPTER NINE

Legions

of

Lost

Ships

*W*hen the wind blows force four or better along the stormy, bleak Outer Banks at Cape Hatteras, then let the sailor beware, for here, off the dreaded Diamond Shoals, where the warm Gulf Stream collides in awesome fury with the cold North Atlantic, "the Lord maketh a deep to boil like a pot." Seafaring men call it the Graveyard of the Atlantic, and it is aptly named, for the miles of towering waves that shoot their spume a hundred feet into the air, the innumerable swirling, sucking maelstrom currents, and the multitude of fanglike shifting sandbars along the entire North Carolina coast have for more than four centuries snared countless ships and doomed hundreds of unwary mariners. Sailing ships, steamships, freighters, tankers, pleasure boats—the angry ocean has cast them all up indiscriminately on the shoals where their rusty remains stand as mute reminders to mariners—"Stay clear of Hatteras."

But not only Hatteras, for this warning applies to the whole North Carolina coast from Cape Fear and the fearful Frying Pan Shoals on the south, up the curving coast to Cape Lookout, then along the treacherous concave arc of the shoal-splined Outer Banks, past Ocracoke, Chicamacomico, Bodie Island, Nag's Head, Kill Devil Hills, and Kitty Hawk, to Currituck Beach in the north—infamous names that have marked the resting places of a legion of lost ships. How many? No one knows for sure, but estimates have ranged from six hundred to well over two thousand.

The question is, Why did a seventeenth-century Spanish frigate en route from Central America to Spain sail a thousand miles out of its way to end by being pounded to pieces in the surf on Diamond Shoals? And why did an English brigantine of the eighteenth century sailing from Great Britain to New York take such a circuitous route to suffer a similar fate on the treacherous sands of Ocracoke Bar?

The answers to these questions lie in the course of the Gulf Stream and in the habits of the early navigators. Even before our coasts were settled by the first Europeans, the Spanish learned that on the way home from the Caribbean they could make better time by taking advantage of the northward flow of the Gulf Stream as it moved up the coast from the Florida Straits at speeds up to five miles an hour, then veered northeastward at Cape Hatteras toward Europe. Although this mighty current is 50 miles wide and 1,500 feet deep, early mariners were reluctant to stray far from known landmarks. For this reason Spanish treasure fleets leaving Cuba sailed directly toward the Florida Keys and purposely skirted the treacherous Florida reefs on their northward journey with the stream, unwittingly risking the storms that could so easily blow them off course to their destruction on the shoals. It was just such a tempest in 1750 that struck the coast-hugging flotilla of Don Juan Manuel de Bonilla, homeward bound for Spain, and scattered the vessels across the Graveyard all the way from Currituck to Topsail Inlet.

Halfway to Europe the Gulf Stream splits. One arm drifts north and east toward the Arctic; the other turns south to join the North Equatorial Current off the hump of Africa. It was this circuitous southward route that all vessels followed when bound for our hemisphere. They sailed down the coast of Africa to the Canary Islands, then followed the Equatorial Current to the West Indies, where they entered the Gulf Stream and let it carry them northward to their destinations on the east coast of the United States. Those that strayed too close to Cape Hatteras through negligence, oversight, or because they were blown off course in a storm, added their hulks to the growing Graveyard of the Atlantic.

Among the many stories of shipwrecks, tragedies, and acts of heroism along the North Carolina coast, two accounts are particularly interesting because of the unusual circumstances surrounding them. One of the most intriguing concerns the schooner *Patriot.* These are the few known facts concerning her fate: The former New York pilot boat sailed from Georgetown, South Carolina, December 30, 1812, bound for New York. Among the passengers was twenty-nine-year-old Theodosia Burr Alston, wife of Governor John Alston of South Carolina and daughter of former Vice President Aaron Burr. The day the ship left port the young woman was said to have been in ill health, for she had recently lost her only child. It is also believed that she was still depressed by the public stigma that surrounded her family name as a result of her father's disgraceful duel with Alexander Hamilton eight years earlier.

Somewhere between South Carolina and New York the *Patriot* vanished. An extensive search was made, but no trace of the ship or survivors was found. It was known only that at the time the schooner was scheduled to pass Cape Hatteras, a severe storm had hit that area. It was presumed that the *Patriot* had been caught in it and all aboard had perished at sea.

There the matter rested until 1833, when an Alabama newspaper reported the deathbed confession of a man who said that he had participated in the capture of the *Patriot,* the murder of everyone aboard, and the scuttling of the schooner "for the sake of her plate [coins] and effects." He was the first of three men who confessed to the murders.

Fifteen years later another deathbed confession from a known pirate revealed that one of the women who had been murdered aboard the *Patriot* was named Odessa Burr Alston.

In 1833 Dr. William G. Pool was treating one of his patients on the Outer Banks when he noticed a remarkable painting of a young woman hanging on the wall of the shack. When he inquired about the portrait, he was told that it had been found aboard a vessel that had beached one morning in January, 1813, about two miles below Nag's Head. According to the account, all the ship's sails were set, the tiller was lashed, and there seemed to be no damage to the craft; yet it was deserted. In the cabin were several fine silk dresses, some waxed flowers, and the portrait. Since Dr. Pool had admired the portrait, the impoverished patient later gave it to him to pay her bill.

In the years that followed, there were many rumors about the fate of the *Patriot*. One was a widely believed account by Charles Gayarre, who wrote a book in which a chapter was devoted to the confession of another known pirate named Dominique You. According to Gayarre, You admitted being the one who overtook the *Patriot* and murdered Theodosia Burr.

In 1888 a descendant of the Burrs's named Stella E. P. Drake went to Elizabeth City to view Dr. Pool's portrait from the derelict. Later she wrote a letter to the Washington (D.C.) *Post* describing that visit: "As I turned to go through the door, I saw upon the wall above the mantlepiece a portrait of a young woman in white.

" 'That is the picture,' I exclaimed. 'I know it is because it bears a strong resemblance to my sister.' "

But was it a portrait of Theodosia Burr, or only a coincidental resemblance? Did the three pirates finally tell the truth, or were they making final bids for notoriety? If the derelict that drifted ashore in January, 1813, was indeed the *Patriot*, why was this fact not publicized at that time? These questions have never been answered.

Mystery also surrounds the fate of the *Carroll A. Deering*, a five-masted schooner launched at Bath, Maine, in 1919. She was described as a "tremendous sailing ship," measuring 225 feet in length, 44.3 feet across her beam, and weighing 1,879 tons. She left Boston in September, 1920, bound for Buenos Aires. It was on the return trip that disaster struck.

In the first light of dawn on January 31, 1921, the lookout on duty at the Cape Hatteras Coast Guard station was surprised to see a five-masted schooner aground on Diamond Shoals, "with all sails set." Four stations sent out lifeboats but could get no closer than a quarter of a mile from the ship because of rough seas over the shoals. The official report stated that the *Deering* was "driven high up on the shoal . . . in a boiling bed of breakers . . . with all sails standing, as if she had been abandoned in a hurry. She had been stripped of all lifeboats and [there was] no sign of life aboard . . . crew had apparently left in [their] own boats as [the] ladder was hanging over the side."

During the next four days, two Coast Guard cutters and a wrecking tug failed to reach the schooner owing to continued high seas. When she was finally boarded, her seams were found to be badly sprung and her hold full of water. Her steering gear was disabled, charts were strewn around the cabin, and food was set out in the galley, but there was no sign of life aboard.

Rumors of murder, mutiny, and piracy began circulating. But the most convincing supposition was that the *Deering* had encountered a storm off the lower Carolina coast that destroyed her steering gear. As she drifted helplessly toward Diamond Shoals, her eleven crewmen elected to try for shore in her lifeboats. The current proved too strong for them and they were lost at sea. The *Carroll A. Deering* then sailed on alone to her fatal rendezvous at Cape Hatteras, and from that day on she was known as the Ghost Ship of Diamond Shoals.

The North Carolina coast is not the only cemetery of lost ships. The shoals of sand that lie between Muskeget and Tuckernuck Islands off Nantucket, Massachusetts, for example, are constantly shifting position under the influence of ocean currents. Over the years these deadly shoals have claimed some twenty-one hundred ships.

Roughly one thousand miles to the northeast of Cape Hatteras and one hundred miles off the coast of Nova Scotia lies Sable Island— "Graveyard of the North Atlantic." Here the warm Gulf Stream meets the icy Labrador Current, and the result is a witch's brew of shifting sandbars, swirling currents, and soupy fogs that are a navigator's nightmare. Like the eroded rim of a caldron, Sable Island is a treeless crescent of sand twenty-three miles long and scarcely a mile wide. Gnawed by sea and storms, it is constantly changing shape. Its far-reaching hidden shoals have caused more than five hundred shipwrecks and taken thousands of lives.

Across the North Atlantic, at Dogger Bank in the North Sea, is another burial ground of lost ships, which is called the Cemetery. Here during northerly or northwesterly gales, just to the leeward of the famous fishing bank, the seas pile up on submerged cliffs to create a roaring welter of waves and crosscurrents feared by all fishermen. On a bitter-cold day early in March, 1883, the Cemetery reaped its single greatest toll in a matter of hours. Shortly before midnight a howling gale struck a fleet of sailing trawlers fishing the northeastern edge of the Dogger Bank. Men were swept from decks; sails, masts, and bulwarks were ripped away. Ships were bowled over or literally burst open by the giant waves. By morning the Cemetary had claimed forty-five trawlers and the lives of 225 men and boys. North Sea fishermen are a hardy lot, but it is said that many of those who saw and survived the wrath of the Cemetery that night never dared face the sea again.

Off Iceland is an area known as the Blinders—uncharted rocks which have been responsible for sinking more trawlers than two world wars. Near the Lofoten Islands of Norway is the malevolent *Moskenstraumen*, said to be the worst four-and-a-half-mile coastal passage in the world. So powerful are the currents there that ships ten miles distant have had to steer four points off their compass course to counteract their pull. A smaller but no less fearful maelstrom called the *Coirebrechan* lies near Scotland's Isle of Jura, while to the north, in the Pentland Firth, racing riptides compress in a fury of dancing waves to create the fearsome phenomena called the Merry Men of Mey, an epithet perhaps derived ironically from the gay dances with which the Scots celebrated May Day. On the east coast of England off Norfolk County, facing the full fury of the North Sea, are the dreaded Haisborough Sand and Hammond's Knoll. These shoals have been responsible for so many shipwrecks that mariners call the area the Devil's Throat. To the southeast, about five miles off the Kentish coast near Deal, lie the treacherous Goodwin Sands, the burial ground for scores of ships, including an entire fleet of treasure-laden Spanish galleons. And off the southern coast of Japan there is a maritime graveyard called the Devil's Sea that is noted for swallowing ships without leaving a trace.

In the days of sail, wherever ships foundered, there were landsmen along the coast quick to take advantage of the mariners' misfortunes. They were called wreckers, or mooncussers because of their dislike for practicing their ghoulish trade in the moonlight. These men, who often operated in gangs, were professionals in the barbaric but profitable business of ship plundering along hazardous coasts such as those of North Carolina, where between 1893 and 1899 an average of almost one ship a week was stranded. However, if business was slow, the wreckers helped it along by setting false lights on shore to lure ships onto the shoals. Nag's Head Beach, North Carolina, got its name from the wreckers' quaint habit of hanging a lantern around a "nag's head" and walking the horse inland, away from an approaching vessel. Ships sighting the distant "beacon" were often led to their destruction before their crews realized what had happened. Once a vessel was aground, the wreckers swarmed over it like sea lice, ransacking and looting. Corpses that washed ashore were immediately robbed of their valuables, while injured survivors were quickly dispatched and then robbed. In their impatience for loot, the wreckers sometimes cut off the fingers of hapless seafarers to get their rings.

In his excellent book, *Sailors Sailors,* published by Paul Hamlyn Ltd. (London, 1966), George Goldsmith-Carter points out that the earliest known law dealing with shipwrecks in Britain is found in the Magna Charta. It reads: "Concerning wrecks of the sea: it is agreed that where a man, a dog, a cat escapes quick [i.e., alive] out of the ship, that ship or barge or anything within them shall not be adjudged as wreck but shall be saved and kept by view of the Coroner, Sheriff or King's Bailiff and delivered into the hands of such of the town where the goods were found. . . . "

Needless to say, with these rights spelled out so clearly, wreckers saw to it that nothing *did* escape alive.

Goldsmith-Carter graphically describes mooncussers at work in a famous graveyard of ships on England's southwestern coast: "Among the most merciless wreckers were the wolf-wild, poverty-stricken tin-miners of the Cornish coast of England. Many of the mines were sited on the high cliffs of the coast of Cornwall and from these rugged eyries the ragged, half-starved miners kept close watch on passing ships. When they saw a vessel in distress and driving shorewards, they ran along the cliff tops, collecting more of their savage kind as they went. Then they gathered like carrion eaters and just waited for the ship to run ashore. Survivors were dealt with swiftly and in a variety of ways — stabbed, held down to drown in the frothing backwash, or beaten on the head with rocks. The ship was then swiftly looted, and as swiftly dismantled within a few hours. So skillful were the wreckers at this that, within a very short time, not a plank or a rope's end remained to mark the spot. The victims were stripped naked and hurled headlong into a hole dug in the beach.

Finally, the wreckers dispersed to fight over their plunder."

The macabre business of wrecking died a natural death with the sailing ship. Engine-powered vessels with better navigational instruments were less often wrecked. And when lifeboat stations sprang up along the most dangerous coasts, wrecking soon became a thing of the past.

Not all ships, however, ended up in coastal graveyards. Many met disaster in storms, or by colliding with icebergs or unknown objects far out at sea. While some of these vessels sank on the spot, others were destined to drift wherever the winds and currents carried them. Once they were caught in the great transoceanic currents used by vessels sailing from America to Europe and back again, these derelicts moved from continent to continent, sometimes approaching, sometimes retreating, and sometimes colliding with other ships hurrying along the same sea routes. For some derelicts, these aimless voyages lasted more than twenty years.

No seafaring man of the late 1800's dared guess where the derelicts came from or where they went, but it was well known that they were there and that the ghostly fleet was growing. The *Marborough*, a three-masted schooner, left New Zealand for England early in January, 1890. The ship was last reported in the Straits of Magellan, but she never reached her destination. The derelict was sighted and boarded again in October, 1913 — twenty-four years later. The *Wyer G. Sargent,* an American merchantman, was abandoned near Cape Hatteras in March, 1891. In December, 1892, she was sighted off Gibraltar. The derelict had covered six thousand miles in 615 days. About the same time, off Cape Horn, the three-master *Emilie Galline* reported sighting a derelict encased in ice. Off the Uruguayan coast, a Spanish trading vessel, the *Josefa,* sighted the magnificent five-master *France,* abandoned and capsized. And there were others. Of the 957 floating wrecks sighted on the Atlantic Ocean between 1887 and 1891, no more than 332 were recognized; 625 of the derelicts had capsized. Of the 1,628 encountered from 1891 to 1893, only 428 could be named.

The dangers of such a fleet in the shipping lanes were at first obvious only to those who sailed. The reasons for the growing list of ships that were mysteriously lost at sea may not have been understood at the time, but later it was realized that many of these vessels had collided with members of this ghostly armada and had either sunk or become drifting hulks themselves.

By the mid-1800's naval authorities were well aware of the hazards posed by the derelicts. They sought and destroyed them at every opportunity, but it was a long, tedious battle. By 1912 the ghost fleet was estimated to be growing at the rate of two hundred ships a year. At the end of 1916, the Navy was ordered to cease its struggle against derelicts because the United States was preparing for another struggle of graver consequence. After World War I, the search for derelicts continued. In 1930 the Coast Guard destroyed 267 floating wrecks; yet even at this rate it was not until we were approaching World War II that the sea lanes were relatively free of these drifting dangers.

Long before the day of the derelict drew to a close, however, the world was to puzzle over one of the most publicized sea mysteries of all time: the fate of the *Mary Celeste.*

On November 5, 1872, the 232-ton brigantine *Mary Celeste* left New York bound for Genoa, with a cargo of sixteen hundred casks of alcohol. On board was her part-owner, thirty-seven-year-old Captain Benjamin Briggs, a stern-faced, strait-laced New Englander of Puritan stock; his wife and baby daughter; and seven crew men.

For seventeen days the brigantine held her course across the North Atlantic, until 8:00 A.M., November 25, 1872, when it was noted on her deck slate log that she passed to the north of Santa Maria Island in the Azores. After that, something strange happened to the *Mary Celeste.*

Eleven days later, in the early afternoon of December 5, the British brigantine *Dei Gratia,* nineteen days out of New York bound for Gibraltar, sighted a sailing vessel east of the Azores. She was heading west, her short canvas oddly set. One sail seemed to be in tatters. Captain Morehouse of the *Dei Gratia* noted that the ship was sailing peculiarly but could see no one on deck.

He altered course to speak to the vessel. When no one answered his calls, the captain sent out his mate and two crewmen in a small boat to investigate. As the seamen approached, they saw the name of the vessel—*Mary Celeste.* Climbing aboard, they found the ship deserted but undamaged. Her standing rigging (stays, shrouds, etc., which secure the masts) was intact. "But the running rigging [ropes with which sails are

TEXT CONTINUED ON PAGE 134

Oliver Deveau, first mate of the British brigantine Dei Gratia, *sailed the abandoned derelict* Mary Celeste *to port.*

This wood engraving shows the Mary Celeste *sailing west toward the Azores without a soul on board. In this condition the* Dei Gratia's *men found and boarded her on December 5, 1872.*

To this day no one has satisfactorily solved the mystery of the Mary Celeste, *in which the captain, Benjamin Spooner Briggs (above), his wife and son, and a crew of seven vanished without a trace while bound from New York to Genoa.*

raised, lowered, or trimmed, booms and gaffs are operated, etc.] was in very bad order and some carried away. The foresail and upper foretopsail had apparently blown from the yards, and the lower foretopsail was hanging by the four corners. The main staysail was hauled down and lying on the forward house as if it had been run down. Jib and foretop staysail set. All the rest of the sails were furled."[1] The masts and spars were intact, the cargo of alcohol seemed in good shape,[2] the forward hatch and cabin skylight were open, and all six of the cabin windows had been boarded up with canvas and plank. There was a foot of water in the cabin, but the ship's hull was sound. The captain's charts lay on the unmade bed. The logbook showed that the last entry had been made eleven days earlier. There was enough food in the galley to last six months. The crew's pipes, tobacco, and belongings were in their quarters. Everything appeared to be in order except that the ship's chronometer, sextant, navigation books, registry papers, and a small deck boat were missing; the ship was sailing in the opposite direction to which she had been going; and the ten human beings who had been aboard had all disappeared.

Thus began one of our greatest sea mysteries. The crew of the *Dei Gratia* sailed the derelict six hundred miles to Gibraltar, where they claimed and eventually received salvage money. But what happened aboard the ship between the last log entry on November 25 and the day she was found sailing back toward home on December 5? What became of the captain, his family, and the crew?

Many books have been written in an attempt to answer those questions. In the process, facts have been altered, added, or subtracted to suit the authors' purposes. There have been tales of murder, piracy, and conspiracy, but no one has yet accounted for all the known facts. A thorough examination of the ship by a board of inquiry at Gibraltar in 1873 produced no evidence of foul play. From testimony given during this inquiry before the Vice Admiralty Court, the most logical explanation for the disappearance of the people aboard seems to be this one:

[1] Testimony of the *Dei Gratia*'s mate, Oliver Deveau, presented on March 4, 1873, to the Vice Admiralty Court sitting at Gibraltar.
[2] ". . . except for one cask that had started [cracked]." Testimony of the shipping surveyor after examining the *Mary Celeste* at Gibraltar.

Early in the morning of November 25, something happened aboard the *Mary Celeste* to convince the experienced Captain Briggs that he must immediately abandon ship. It may have been something to do with his highly volatile cargo of alcohol—perhaps the discovery of fumes from a leaking cask in the hold; the fear of a sudden explosion. Whatever the reason, the captain, his family, and the crew left the ship in the one small boat, possibly intending to pull off at a safe distance to wait and see what happened. A sudden gust of wind filled the few sails that remained set and the brigantine lurched away from them, gaining more speed than they had anticipated. Try as they might, the crew could not row fast enough to overtake the rapidly moving ship. Finally, totally exhausted, there they sat in their small boat, numb with shock as they realized that without food or water they could not long survive. And in the distance, the *Mary Celeste* sailed on to become one of the eternal unexplained mysteries of the sea.

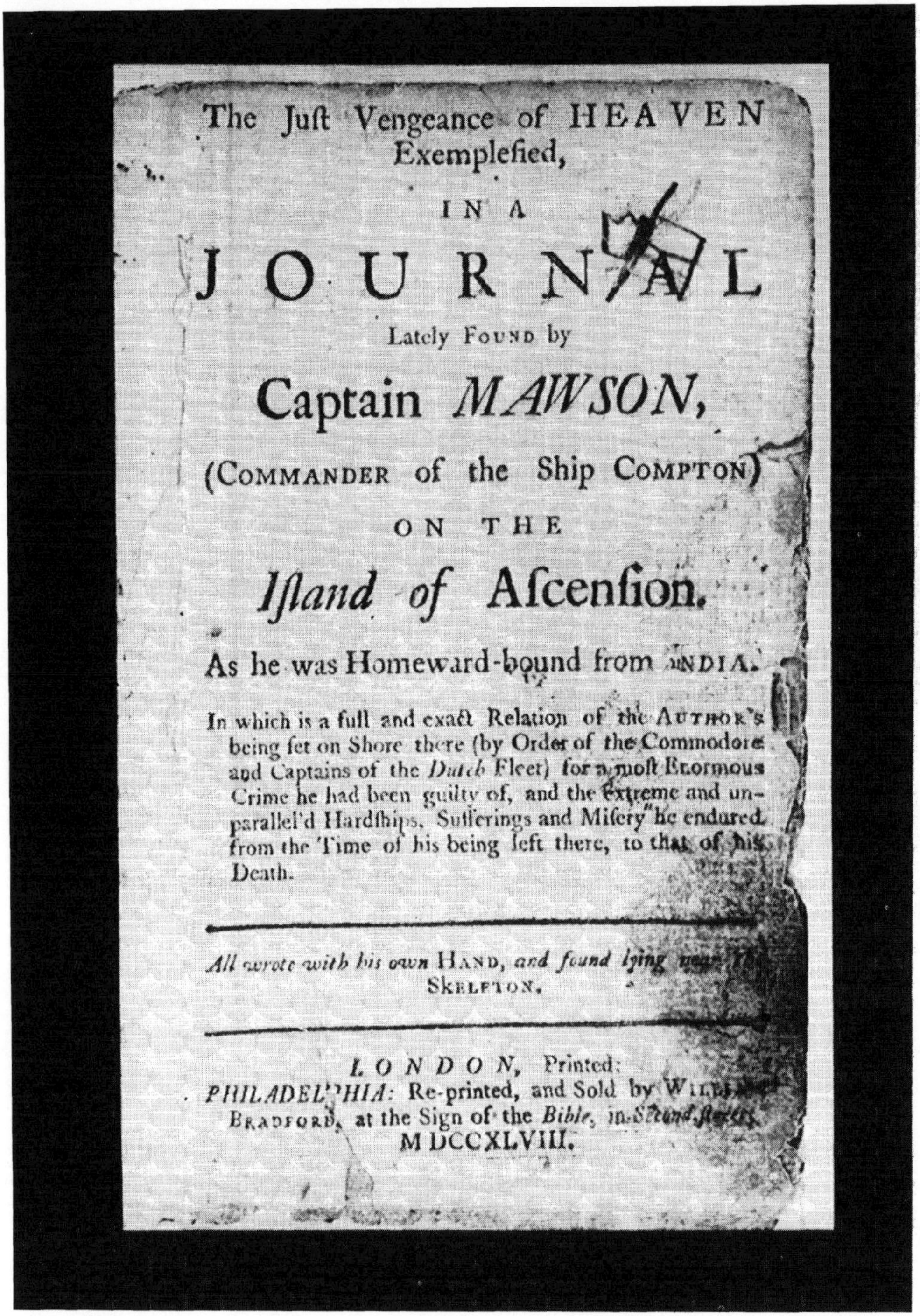

The Juſt Vengeance of HEAVEN
Exemplefied,

IN A

JOURNAL

Lately Found by

Captain MAWSON,

(COMMANDER of the Ship COMPTON)

ON THE

Iſland of Aſcenſion.

As he was Homeward-bound from INDIA.

In which is a full and exact Relation of the AUTHOR's
being ſet on Shore there (by Order of the Commodore
and Captains of the Dutch Fleet) for a moſt Enormous
Crime he had been guilty of, and the extreme and un-
parallel'd Hardſhips, Sufferings and Miſery he endured
from the Time of his being left there, to that of his
Death.

All wrote with his own HAND, and found lying near
SKELETON.

LONDON, Printed:
PHILADELPHIA: Re-printed, and Sold by WILLIAM
BRADFORD, at the Sign of the Bible, in Second Street.
MDCCXLVIII.

The title page of the memoirs left by the nameless castaway on Ascension Island

CHAPTER TEN

The

Fate of

Castaways

No book on shipwrecks would be complete without a mention of the victims—the castaways— whose luck in surviving the initial disaster often led them to a far grimmer fate adrift on seaborne wreckage or marooned on deserted islands. All mariners risk an accident of this kind each time they go to sea, but in the early days of sail it was more than a remote possibility that men would be deliberately set adrift by pirates, mutineers, or disgruntled sea captains. Such was the fate of an unidentified seaman who was put ashore on Ascension Island in 1725 for "an enormous crime he had been guilty of."

Ascension is a desolate volcanic island thirty-four miles square that lies alone in the South Atlantic, midway between Africa and South America. Captain Mawson, commander of the ship *Compton,* was homeward bound from India when he stopped there and found the remains of a campsite, the sun-bleached bones of a human skeleton, and beside them a diary, which detailed the unfortunate author's final hardships.

The diary began: "By order of the commodore and captains of the Dutch Fleet I was set on shore the 5th of May, 1725, upon the island of Ascension, which struck me with great dread and uneasiness, having no hopes remaining but that the Almighty God would be my protector. They put on shore with me a cask of water, a hatchet, two buckets, an old frying pan, a fowling piece, teakettle, tarpaulin, onions, pease, calivances,[1] rice, etc. I pitched my tent on the sand near a rock, that I might better know where to find them again. . . ."

During the first few days the castaway described how he explored the barren island in the hope of finding game, and how he managed to kill three sea birds. On May 7 he accidentally tipped over his cask of water, losing much of it. His rifle was useless because he had neither powder nor shot, so he used it to support a distress flag he made from a white shirt. Meanwhile he made daily trips to a promontory, searching for a sail on the horizon. One day he found some wild greens and roots, which he cooked and ate. Another day he killed a seaturtle and dined royally, salting and sun-curing some of the flesh. A month later he was down to his last two quarts of water, which was "so thick that I was obliged to strain it through my handkerchief." He tried digging a well, but gave it up after reaching a depth of seven feet without finding the slightest trace of moisture. As his food supplies dwindled, he searched the island for anything edible. He found a small trickle of fresh water but almost nothing to eat. He was finally reduced to living on a stew of rice and weeds. His shoes wore out. During the scorching days he prayed constantly, while at night his sleep was disturbed by loud noises and cursing voices, which he attributed to evil spirits trying to torment him. On June 29 he drank the last of his water. The next day he found that his trickle of a stream had dried up and he became delirious. By accident he found about a gallon of water in the hollow of a rock, and drinking it sparingly, he regained enough strength to find a few bird's eggs. More pockets of water in the rocks saw him through another month, but by then he had exhausted all there were. He prayed fervently for help but none came. He again killed a sea turtle, eating it raw and drinking its blood. Killing still another, he broke his only usable weapon, a hatchet.

[1] chickpeas.

Four months after he had been cast away, the seaman wrote; "From the 5th to the 8th I lived upon turtle blood and eggs, from the 8th to the 14th I lingered on with no other food to subsist me. I am becoming a moving skeleton, my strength is entirely decayed. I cannot write much longer. I sincerely repent of the sins I committed and pray, henceforth, no man may ever merit the misery which I have undergone. For the sake of which, leaving this narrative behind me to deter mankind from following such diabolical inventions. I now resign my soul to him that gave it, hoping for mercy in . . ."

There the diary ended.

Other island castaways have been more fortunate. In the western Caribbean, two hundred miles off the coast of Nicaragua, there is a small, barren, horseshoe-shaped, sand-and-rock reef called the Serrana Bank. It was named for Pedro Serrano, the sole survivor of a ship wrecked off the island in 1528. Incredibly, he survived on this treeless, waterless, deserted cay for eight years until he was rescued.

Serrano swam ashore without food or clothes. Rain was his only source of water, and this he supplemented by drinking the blood of turtles and birds. For two years he ate raw what animals he could catch. Then one day he dived down to the shipwreck and found a flint. After that he was able to build a fire and cook his food. During Serrano's third year another ship struck the reef and its lone survivor swam ashore. The castaways built two stone towers on which they kept driftwood fires burning in the hope that a passing ship would sight them.

When rescue finally came, the excitement proved too great for Serrano's companion, who died after a few days at sea. Serrano, however, returned to Spain, where he was treated like a celebrity. With his hair and beard reaching almost to his knees and wearing sharkskins he had sewn into clothes, he traveled throughout the royal courts of Europe, arousing the sympathy of all who saw him and heard his tale.

With few exceptions, the worst fate to befall a sailor is to be cast away at sea in an open boat. Those who have survived have had terrible tales to tell. One of the most famous open-boat voyages took place in 1789, when the *Bounty* mutineers set Captain William Bligh and eighteen of his crew adrift in a provisioned launch while the *Bounty* sailed on to Tahiti. The castaways, sustained by the bitter vindictiveness of their captain, astonished everyone by rowing and sailing 3,618 miles to Timor, near Java.

Less fortunate was the crew of the whaling vessel *Essex,* which was attacked by an enraged eighty-five-foot sperm whale in the South Pacific in 1819. The whale smashed in the ship's heavy timbers with its head, and the vessel sank so quickly that the crew barely had time to take to the small boats and get clear. The boats finally became separated and were repeatedly attacked by sharks. When their meager food supplies ran out, the starving men were reduced to cannibalism. Three survivors were picked up by the English brig *India.* Then, three months later the skipper, Captain Pollard, and a crew member were found more dead than alive by the whaling ship *Dauphin.* The story of the *Essex* was the basis for a similar disastrous encounter between a ship and a whale described in Herman Melville's classic, *Moby Dick.*

Reading early accounts of open-boat castaways one is struck by the number of times that survivors resorted to cannibalism. In *Great Shipwrecks and Castaways,* the author, Charles Neider, relates several of these gruesome occurrences. One involved the survivors of a herring boat that sank in a storm off the Maine coast on the afternoon of July 22, 1904. Of ten crewmen, only three managed to reach a small lifeboat. They were Jeb Cannon, Clem Mallory, and James Thomas. They had no food or water. A widespread search for them proved fruitless.

A month later Jeb Cannon was picked up by a herring boat. His brown hair had turned gray; his face was blackened by the sun. He had survived by catching rainwater in his shirt and wringing it out into a bailing can. In the lifeboat were large chunks of meat—the remains of James Thomas—which he had been eating. When Cannon was taken aboard the herring boat, he became hysterical. Once he had been soothed with rum, he related that first Mallory and then Thomas had died of exposure, and that he had eaten them to stay alive.

Fourteen years later, on his deathbed, Cannon revealed what had actually happened. He said that the three of them had drifted for days without food, slowly starving to death. About two weeks after the shipwreck, Cannon shot Mallory through the head with a pistol he had salvaged. He ordered Thomas to cut up the body so they could eat. When his weak companion only glared at him and mumbled incoherently, Cannon did the grisly job himself. He ate for several days until the meat spoiled and had to be thrown away. From then on, Cannon slept with a tight grip on his pistol. Three days before he was rescued, he had shot Thomas.

When Cannon's neighbors heard the dying man's confession, they were so incensed that they refused to give him a decent burial. Instead they rowed his corpse out to sea and dumped it overboard.

*   *   *

On June 4, 1923, the British tramp steamer *Trevessa* sank in a violent storm in the mid-Indian Ocean. Before she went down, her forty-eight officers and crewmen crowded into two lightly provisioned lifeboats and took to the sea. Each twenty-six-foot boat carried nine gallons of water, six tins of biscuits, and 130 tins of condensed milk. Daily rations consisted of two tablespoonfuls of condensed milk, one tablespoonful of water, and one biscuit per man. After five days of sailing before the wind, it became apparent that they would not soon be rescued. The water ration was cut in half. Since one lifeboat was able to travel faster than the other, they separated.

Twelve days after the ordeal began, the first man died and was buried at sea. Others followed periodically. Before long the survivors looked like scarecrows. Their unkempt hair and beards covered shrunken features crusted white with salt. Their sunken eyes were bloodshot, the flesh on their arms had withered, their skin was wrinkled, and their hands were little more than claws. Cracked lips, parched throats, and thick tongues had long since discouraged any attempt at speech. Arid mouths quickly absorbed the meager ration of liquid before it even reached the equally dry throats. Few had the strength to eat. Those who tried to nibble a biscuit ended by blowing it out as powder. Still, the castaways clung stubbornly to life and somehow kept their lifeboat sailing on across the sun-glazed sea.

The faster of the two lifeboats reached land first; then, twenty-five days after abandoning the *Trevessa*, the slower boat arrived with its pitiful cargo. The survivors had traveled an incredible twenty-three hundred miles across the Indian Ocean—one of the longest unbroken voyages ever made in an open boat, and a remarkable tribute to man's will to survive.

*   *   *

By far the most popular account of a castaway's successful survival is contained in Daniel Defoe's *Robinson Crusoe,* a novel inspired by the adventures of a seaman named Alexander Selkirk.

During the War of the Spanish Succession (1701–1714), Selkirk was the sailing master of an English privateer named the *Cinque Ports.* The ship had been involved in numerous engagements with Spanish shipping in the South Pacific and it was badly damaged. Moreover, honest Alexander Selkirk, as one early chronicler called him, had fallen out with his captain, and the "irreconcilable difference" decided the sailing master to leave the shot-riddled vessel at the first opportunity.

That opportunity came early in September, 1704, when the *Cinque Ports* dropped anchor at Juan Fernández,[2] a thirteen-mile-long island that juts out of the southern Pacific like a rock fortress some four hundred miles west off Valparaiso, Chile. Selkirk made no secret of his intentions, and the ship's captain obliged him by landing him and all his belongings as if he were a passenger off on an island vacation. As Selkirk told the story years later, he was, in effect, a voluntary castaway, but he had strong misgivings about his decision the moment he saw the ship sailing off. He waded out up to his chest and begged to be taken back on board again, but the captain had already interpreted Selkirk's conduct as mutinous and decided that exile was a fitting punishment. A few weeks later, the unseaworthy ship surrendered to the Spaniards to avoid a watery grave.

Meanwhile, Selkirk gloomily surveyed his meager possessions: some clothes and bedding, a firelock with powder and bullets, some tobacco, a knife and a hatchet, his nautical instruments, some books, and a Bible. He had no food or water.

His first shelter was a shallow cave, but the nightly roaring of sea lions on the shore forced him to scale the cliffs with his belongings and seek refuge elsewhere.

High in the slopes he built two huts: a small one in which he cooked, and a larger one in which he slept and read. For food he relied mainly on the island's large population of goats. These he easily shot until he ex-

TEXT CONTINUED ON PAGE 146

[2] Also called Más a Tierra.

Robinson Crusoe, having improvised a raft, takes supplies off his wrecked ship.

Based in part on the actual experiences of the marooned sailor Alexander Selkirk, Daniel Defoe's novel The Life and Strange Surprizing Adventures of Robinson Crusoe *was an enormous success when it appeared in 1719. These two illustrations are from the first edition.*

hausted his supply of powder and bullets. After that, he caught them by running them down. Eventually he tamed a few of them so that he would always have a ready supply of meat and milk. When his clothes wore out, he sewed new ones of dried goatskins, perforating the hides with a nail and cutting strips of thong for thread. Turtles and fish did not agree with him, but he enjoyed the clawless lobsters he caught along the rocky coast. Wild palm cabbage substituted for bread, and he found turnips, radishes, and parsnips, planted probably by the same seamen who had introduced the goats with an eye to restocking the stores of passing ships.

Selkirk daily scanned the sea for sign of a sail that might mean his salvation. But in the four years and four months that he was there, only two ships—Spanish frigates—stopped at the island. They arrived together, and when the hostile Spaniards glimpsed the hairy hermit dressed in skins, they chased him. Selkirk swiftly outdistanced his pursuers and climbed a leafy tree until they gave up and sailed away.

Other ships passed the island without seeing or without changing course for Selkirk's signal fires. Finally, on February 1, 1709, the English privateers *Duke* and *Dutchess,* under the command of Captain Woodes Rogers, sailed into the bay. Selkirk raced to kindle a fire on the beach and spent the night beside it while the ships lay at anchor. Rogers, fearing a trap, waited until noon the next day before dispatching a boat to investigate. The well-armed seamen were astounded by the wild-looking apparition in animal skins who greeted them. When they took Selkirk aboard the *Duke,* Captain Rogers was not sure what manner of man confronted him. He said that the castaway had "so much forgot his Language for want of Use, that we could scarce understand him, for he seem'd to speak his words by halves."

To Captain Rogers' habit of keeping a journal we owe the earliest account of Selkirk's experiences as a castaway. Rogers reported that he offered Selkirk a dram of rum "but he would not touch it, having drank nothing but water since his being there, and 't was some time before he could relish our victuals." The captain had a bulldog, which he sent ashore with his fastest runners to help capture goats. But Selkirk "distanced and tired both the dog and men, catching goats, and brought 'em to us on his back." His feet were so calloused from racing over the rocky island that it was a long time before he could wear shoes again.

Rogers' ships spent ten days taking on provisions at the island, then headed north to prey on enemy shipping. Selkirk was made master of the second Spanish ship they captured. For the next eleven months the privateers attacked and looted vessels from Chile to Mexico, amassing a large amount of gold and silver bullion. By the time they had circled the globe and sailed home to England, Selkirk was no longer a poor castaway but a comparatively wealthy man from his share of the booty. He disembarked near London in mid-October, 1711, and went home to Largo, Scotland, dressed in gold-laced finery.

What happened to Selkirk after that is not clear. The quiet little town of Largo could hardly have been as dull as the life he had known on the island, yet it seems that his need for solitude was so ingrained that he found civilized living too lively for his taste. It is said that he often roamed by himself in the woods and was heard to lament: "Oh, my beloved island! I wish I had never left thee!"

He built a small cavelike shelter in his father's garden, and when he was not inside it he could usually be found strolling the fields or the shore alone. The people of Largo began to avoid the shy man, but apparently not all of them did, for Selkirk eloped with a Largo girl named Sophia Bruce. The pair was traced to London, where Sophia was found alone. Selkirk, like all good sailors, had gone back to the sea. The records show that several years later he was "mate of His Majesty's ship, *Weymouth*" and died aboard that vessel off the coast of Africa in 1721.

The restless castaway never returned to his "beloved island," but today, two thousand feet above sea level on Juan Fernández, near a place that Selkirk called his lookout, a handsome tablet reads:

In memory of ALEXANDER SELKIRK, *mariner, a native of Largo, in the county of Fife, Scotland, who lived on this island in complete solitude for four years and four months. He was landed from the* Cinque Ports *galley, 96 tons, 18 guns,* A.D. *1704, and was taken off in the* Duke, *privateer, 12th February, 1709. He died Lieutenant of H.M.S.* Weymouth, A.D. *1721, aged 47. This tablet is erected near Selkirk's lookout, by Commodore Powell and the officers of H.M.S.* Topaze, A.D. *1868.*

As early as 1888 the riverboat era attracted artists in search of romantic subjects.

CHAPTER ELEVEN

Shipwrecks
of the
Great Lakes
and Rivers

Nowhere on earth are there freshwater seas as vast as the five Great Lakes. The combined shorelines of lakes Ontario, Erie, Huron, Superior, and Michigan total 8,300 miles and enclose 94,710 square miles of water. Anyone who has ever lived near the lakes can tell you about the weather there. When the fog rolls in, every adjective ever used to describe it would fit those undulating walls of gray, and the moan of the Great Lakes foghorns is unforgettable. The lakes breed some of the most vicious storms in the world. Powerful gales can spring up with little or no warning, whipping the water into steep, short-spaced Matterhorn waves that have swamped or broken the back of many a vessel unlucky enough to be caught in them. Many of the ships have gone down with millions of dollars worth of salvageable cargo—copper, steel billets, locomotives, iron ore, and in some cases, gold and silver bullion. Thanks to these disasters, the Great Lakes have their share of legends about lost ships. Perhaps the most famous of all is the mysterious disappearance of the *Griffin*.

In 1679 the famous French explorer Robert Cavelier, Sieur de La Salle, built the forty-ton vessel from hand-hewn logs cut in the forests of New York. She was to be a supply ship for an expedition from Montreal, Canada, westward to the unexplored Mississippi River. Her figurehead was carved to resemble a griffin, the mythological Greek monster with the body of a lion and the head and wings of an eagle. On her maiden voyage late in the summer of 1679, the *Griffin* left old Fort Niagara in western New York, sailed down the Niagara River, crossed Lake Erie, and passed through the Detroit Straits. She continued northward on Lake Huron, navigated the treacherous straits of Mackinac into Lake Michigan, and finally anchored in Green Bay to take on a large shipment of pelts from local trappers.

Since La Salle needed additional supplies for his trek westward, he decided to send the *Griffin* and its valuable cargo back to Fort Niagara, where the sale of the hides would provide him with the funds necessary to equip his expedition. He entrusted the ship to his pilot, Luc Dane, who started the return trip across Lake Michigan on September 18, 1679. From that day on, neither ship nor crew were ever heard from again. The mystery of La Salle's missing ship has become a legend of the Great Lakes. Even the Indians wove tales about a ghostly *Griffin* that could be seen on certain stormy nights with all sails set, battling the waves of Lake Michigan.

When I was a youngster, three of my friends and I felt certain that the bones of the *Griffin* lay on the bottom of a spring-fed lake near Lake Michigan. Our reason for this was that the wreck had been snagging fishing lures and anchors longer than any of the local old-timers could remember. The possibility that the *Griffin* had carried treasure was not our primary interest: we were intrigued by the thought of all that fishing tackle.

Since this was before the days of swim fins, face masks, and scuba gear, we decided to have a look at the wreck with homemade diving equipment. This consisted of an ancient fly-wheel air pump connected by fifty feet of air hose to a World War II gas mask with its canister removed. A dozen extension cords allowed us to plug the pump's electric motor into the outlet at a nearby cottage on the cold September day we elected to have our first trial run. The test was a success. I had clutched at the weeds on the bottom of the lake to hold myself five feet under water for fifteen minutes. All we had to do was replace the electric motor with a gasoline engine and we would be ready to dive on the *Griffin* the next summer.

As soon as school was out the following year we were on the lake. We located the wreck by dragging an anchor into it. A weighted rope known as a shot line, which divers used to guide them to and from the bottom, told us that it was in thirty-five feet of water. It had rained the night before and the lake was the color of mustard, but since our anchor had fouled in the wreck, there was nothing to do but go down and free it.

The water was icy and visibility was almost zero as I started down the shot line. At ten feet I was panting and spinning slowly around my line, not entirely certain which way was up or down. A few feet deeper and there was an excruciating pain in my ears. Water pressure was squeezing my inner ear and sinus passages out of shape, but since I did not know how to correct it by snorting air and equalizing the pressure, I continued down. My ears popped, the pain vanished, and I wondered if I had broken my eardrums. The rest of the trip to the bottom was uneventfully terrifying as the light gradually faded from mustard yellow to murky brown.

Finally my feet touched what turned out to be the tilted transom of a large wooden ship. The deck was gone and long spikes protruded inward around the perimeter of the hull. The spikes were covered with brittle encrustations that came off in my hands, leaving slender cores of sharp steel. I tried lowering myself into the ship's hold, but when I could not feel the bottom, I thought better of it. I climbed out and worked my way around the gunwale. The wreck was about sixty feet long. It was pitched partway over on its beam-ends with its stern in deeper water than its bow. Lying diagonally across the hull was a mast the size of a telephone pole. By silhouetting it against the brown twilight overhead, I could dimly see what looked like floating shroudlines. When I touched one of them, it dissolved in my hand. Then I realized that it was one of many anchor ropes that entangled the wreck. When I ran my hand along the mast, I knew I had found the real prize: it was festooned with fishing lures. I loaded up with loot, salvaged some massive mooring rings, spikes, and a chunk of the hull as souvenirs, then surfaced.

Since I had been gone for thirty minutes, my salvage partners were pleased to see me, especially after I showed them the lures. I had a bloody nose and a cut knee, but my eardrums were intact. Of course we had not found the *Griffin,* but it did not really matter. The dive had been a success, and we were sure that we had found far more practical treasure than La Salle's old ship would have offered us anyway.

While there is undoubtedly a fortune to be salvaged from the Great Lakes, conditions are far from perfect. The wrecks are frequently buried beneath tons of sand or protected by treacherous rocks and strong undercurrents. Moreover, the Great Lakes are deep and extremely cold. Their maximum depths are as follows: Lake Erie, 216 feet; Lake Ontario, 802 feet; Lake Huron, 750 feet; Lake Michigan, 923 feet; and Lake Superior, 1,333 feet.

Despite these difficulties, however, salvage operations have taken place. The story of the steamer *Erie* is typical. On August 9, 1841, the *Erie* left New York and started across Lake Erie carrying three hundred German and Norwegian immigrants who had with them an estimated $100,000 for purchasing land on which they planned to settle in Wisconsin. Four miles off Silver Creek, New York, a fire swept the ship, and she sank, taking the crew and passengers to the bottom.

In 1854 a Buffalo firm, using suited divers, found the *Erie* and blasted her open. But of the reputed $100,000, records show that the divers recovered only $2,000 in coins and some sixty tons of broken machinery.

In 1960 a group of skin divers equipped with scuba gear located the wreck again and in five dives recovered some $1,200 worth of rubles, marks, kroner, and English sovereigns. If there is more treasure to be found, it undoubtedly lies scattered beneath the shifting sands of Lake Erie in forty-eight feet of water.

One point in favor of any salvage operation on the Great Lakes is that wrecks deteriorate considerably more slowly than they do in tropical seas. Wooden vessels, for example, are not attacked by destructive shipworms, as Frank Hoffman, a forty-one-year-old scuba diver from Egg Harbor, Wisconsin, discovered. In 1967 he came across the wreck of a large two-masted schooner resting on the bottom of Green Bay in 110 feet of water. For two years Hoffman and a dozen other divers worked to salvage the ship. From murky depths where the water temperature was only a few degrees above freezing, the men brought up coins and other artifacts. In winter, when the bay froze over, they searched old newspapers until they established the ship's identity. She was the *Alvin Clark,* which sank on June 29, 1864. The divers pumped the silt out of the hull of the wreck, ran cables under it, and brought it to the surface on July 29, 1969. The 110-foot wooden vessel was virtually undamaged after lying on the bottom of Lake Michigan for over a century.

*   *   *

In the past the great rivers of the world were the highways of continental exploration, just as today they are the arteries of commerce.

Their development is as rich in stories of ships and shipwrecks as the history of any sea. Of the great North American rivers, the mighty Mississippi has had the most colorful past.

Springing from a trickle in Minnesota, it swells to a wide, lazy waterway that undulates from north to south for 3,710 miles through the heartland of America. Showboats, steamboats, and riverboat gamblers were an integral part of that fabulous era before the Civil War, when at night river traffic was composed of "floating palaces of steamers that frequently look like living moving mountains of light and flame, so brilliantly are the enormous leviathans illuminated outside and inside . . . steamer after steamer coming, sweeping, sounding, thundering on. . . ."

Steamboat companies competed so fiercely to provide better schedules and faster service that poor construction, improper maintenance, and disastrous fires contributed to the death of most of the vessels before they had served for five years. In the course of their passing, they took a heavy toll of lives. Between 1810 and 1850, riverboat accidents on the Mississippi alone caused the death of more than four thousand persons. One of the most tragic disasters involved the famous old steamboat *Sultana.*

On a mild spring day in April, 1865, at Vicksburg, Mississippi, a large group of soldiers from the victorious Union army waited for the steamboat *Sultana,* which was to take them to St. Louis, on the first leg of their long trip home. In their tattered blue uniforms the soldiers did not look like victors. Most of them were wounded, wasted, and sick men who had spent two years in the Confederate prison camp at Chaba, Alabama.

For two days they had waited patiently on the docks at Vicksburg.

In April, 1865, disastrously overloaded, the venerable steamboat
Sultana *left Vicksburg, Mississippi, for St. Louis. She had been*
built to accommodate about four hundred passengers plus cargo,
but on this trip, in addition to horses, mules, and other goods, she
carried more than 2,000 Union soldiers returning home at the
close of the Civil War. She was so crowded that those aboard were
barely able to find places to stand. Two hours out of Memphis,
her aged boiler exploded, she burst into flame, and 1,450 died.

Then the *Sultana* finally came. In many ways like the sad-faced passengers she was about to take on, the old riverboat was a little the worse for wear. Her once-gleaming white paint was now smoke-begrimed, cracked, and peeling. All her safety equipment had vanished long ago. And the very heart of the old steamboat—her rusty boiler plant—was on the verge of failure.

Despite her condition, the *Sultana* was a welcome sight to the men who pushed and hobbled aboard. Some laughed and smiled for the first time in years. Others cried quietly to themselves. Someone played "Swing Low, Sweet Chariot" on a harmonica, and a few tried to sing. Most of that day the men kept coming and crowding aboard until by sailing time, late that afternoon, there was barely enough room to stand, let alone to sit or lie down. The 1,720-ton *Sultana* had been built to accommodate four hundred passengers and cargo. She now held two thousand ex-prisoners of war, two companies of fully armed infantry, a number of horses and mules, and one hundred hogsheads of sugar. As the heavily overloaded boat slowly pulled away from the dock, she sounded her whistle and it stuck, shrilling loudly for what seemed an eternity. Men whose nerves were already shattered screamed that it was driving them crazy. When someone finally shut off the whistle's steam valve, there was numbing silence. It was as if the old ship had uttered her last piercing cry of defiance.

In the middle of the night, two hours upriver from Memphis, the *Sultana* was laboring her way through a group of islands known locally as the Hens and Chickens when suddenly she was shaken by a tremendous explosion. Hatches blew off, taking men with them. Live steam, escaping below decks, scalded screaming men and animals alike. Clouds of black smoke laced with white steam erupted from every opening. Flames licked up from the engine room. In the turmoil some men began to shoot to protect themselves from being trampled by the crazed horses. Then with a *whoosh* of flames, the entire ship went up. Around the huge burning pyre the river was a mass of flailing arms and bobbing heads lighted grotesquely by the fire. *The Sultana* took the lives of 1,450 soldiers on their way home from war. Although they never reached their destinations, they had perhaps at last found peace.

The excursion steamer General Slocum *sinks after burning in New York's East River.*

CHAPTER TWELVE

Famous

Marine

Disasters

On the morning of June 15, 1904, the trim paddle-wheel steamer *General Slocum* stood ready for boarding at her pier on East Third Street, New York. She was to take fourteen hundred members of the St. Mark's German Lutheran Church on a day's outing and picnic at Locust Point on Long Island Sound.

Shortly after 9:00 A.M. the 250-foot-long boat pulled away from the pier, her flags flying, her band playing a lively German melody, and her three decks crowded to capacity. Women gossiped together while their laughing children chased each other merrily around the ship. The passengers were to be landed about noon at the picnic grounds and returned to New York by 11:00 P.M. The *Slocum* was commanded by Captain William Van Schaick, who had been with her for many years. Assisting him were two pilots and a crew of twenty-three.

When the majestic white steamer backed into the currents and headed upriver, her deep whistle blast was answered by the clanging bells and shrill toots of tugboats. The freshly painted excursion boat with towering twin yellow smokestacks mounted side by side ahead of her huge paddle boxes was a familiar sight along the bustling New York waterfront.

Accounts differ as to the steamer's exact position when disaster struck, but it is certain that she had passed without trouble through the narrow rocky channel between Manhattan and Long Island known as Hell Gate, because people on shore remember hearing sounds of merriment from the ship. When the vessel was about opposite 130th Street in the East River, a fire was discovered in a paint locker in the forward section of the ship. Crewmen hastened up with a fire hose, but it would not work. Vital moments were wasted until someone found that the nozzle had been blocked with a rubber disk to prevent water from dripping on the deck. By the time the disk had been removed, the flames had begun to spread in the breeze created by the ship's headway. When the water pressure was turned up, the rotten hose spouted a dozen leaks, leaving hardly a trickle to fight the blaze.

When the fire was first discovered, the *Slocum* was only three hundred yards from the Manhattan shore, but instead of turning into the wharf, Captain Van Schaick for some unaccountable reason chose to keep up steam and head instead for nearby North Brother Island.

Black smoke and tongues of flame burst out of the forward hatches. There was a muffled explosion, and within seconds the entire forward section of the tinder-dry wooden ship was ablaze. The passengers crowded in panic at the stern of the steamer. Although there seemed to be an ample supply of life preservers, they proved to be as worthless as the fire hoses. The rotten canvas fell to pieces as frantic women fought over them.

As the holocaust swept down on the stern, trapped passengers dropped overboard in scores, many with their clothes on fire. Still the vessel seemed under control as she raced past a smooth sand beach and rounded the point at North Brother Island, where she was run aground on the jagged rocks of a small cove. A worse landing spot could hardly have been selected, for the bow of the vessel was rammed onto the rocks while its crowded stern was still in twenty-five feet of water. Just as the ship struck, the supports of her hurricane deck burned away and the entire upper works came crashing down into the decks below. The shrieks of the injured could be heard by workers on the Bronx shore. By then the *Slocum* was completely enveloped in flames. When the last survivors jumped, the struggling mass of humanity was so thick in the cove that some people were held above water only by the bodies jammed so closely around them. By the time rescuers arrived, the *General Slocum* had burned to her waterline. In less than two hours, one of the worst marine disasters of the century had taken the lives of more than one thousand people, mostly women and children. Captain Van Schaick was arrested and sentenced to ten years in jail, but that could hardly atone for the tragedy that might have been avoided. The only good that came of the disaster was a stringent reappraisal of steamboat inspection laws and broad changes in marine safety regulations.

*   *   *

On the night of April 15, 1912, eight years after the *Slocum* burned, the keen bow of the 46,000-ton superliner *Titanic* knifed through the serene moonlit North Atlantic on her maiden voyage from Southampton, England, to New York. She was a triumph of the shipbuilder's art. A double bottom ran the full length of her 852-foot hull. The hull contained a massive collision bulkhead forward followed by sixteen watertight compartments. Not only was the great ship "unsinkable," but she was a floating palace capable of speeds in excess of twenty-three knots. Her passenger accommodations included private promenade decks, sumptuously furnished suites, cabins, and lounges, a heated swimming pool, a fully equipped gymnasium, and a hospital. She was the pride of the British White Star Line's fleet; the safest, largest, swiftest, and most comfortable ship afloat.

On April 14 the *Titanic* had been warned by radio messages from the *Caronia,* the *Baltic,* the *Mesaba,* and the *Amerika* that there was ice in the sea lanes. Early the following night, the nearby *Californian* reported icebergs dead ahead. But the *Titanic* steamed on at full speed.

At 11:00 P.M. the *Titanic*'s radio operator, who had been working Cape Race, heard the *Californian* break in to report: "We have been stopped by ice."

He answered: "Keep out, you are jamming my signals." The *Californian*'s radio operator then took off his earphones, closed down his station, and went to bed.

Shortly after 11:30 the *Titanic*'s lookout reported an iceberg ahead. Instantly the first officer on the bridge reversed the port engine and put the rudder hard over to make as tight a turn to port as possible. The mighty bow slid safely past the ghostly white mountain of ice, but the ship's momentum carried her forward onto a sharp submerged shoulder that ripped a three-hundred-foot gash in her hull below the waterline on the starboard side. The impact of the collision was so slight that only a few of the engineers and stokers working in the bowels of the ship realized how serious it was.

The captain immediately sent an officer below to survey the damage. Moments later he returned to the bridge with the appalling report that the starboard boiler room had been abandoned; that water rushing into No. 3 hold was already fourteen feet above the keel, and that the ship would sink. The captain ordered the radio operator to request help from nearby ships. Fifty-eight miles away, the *Carpathia* heard the *Titanic*'s SOS, turned, and headed for her at full speed through the ice-strewn sea. The *Virginian*, the *Baltic*, the *Olympic*, and Cape Race also heard. Soon the whole world knew that the *Titanic*, with 2,224 people aboard, was sinking. There was not a chance that any of these vessels could reach the stricken ship before she went down. Ironically, salvation lay only ten miles away, aboard the *Californian*.[1] But her radio was turned off.

While the *Titanic*'s stewards awakened sleeping passengers, helped them with their life jackets, and directed them to lifeboats, her junior officers periodically fired distress rockets from the bridge and signaled with a blinker light in an attempt to attract a rescue vessel. Some of the *Californian*'s crew saw the rockets, but they assumed that they were company identification rockets used by steamships of the era. It was unthinkable that the safest ship afloat could be in trouble.

Meanwhile, the *Titanic*'s first-class passengers were reluctant to leave the warmth and security of the upper decks for the discomfort of a lifeboat in the icy, forbidding sea, and the first boat to be lowered was

---

[1] When she learned of the disaster in the morning, the *Californian* plowed through the ice field and arrived at the scene in two hours.

only partially filled. But below decks, closer to the rising water, hundreds of immigrants were fearfully aware of the urgency to leave, yet were unable to get to the boats. Few passengers realized that the *Titanic's* lifeboats would hold fewer than half the people aboard.

By 2:05 A.M., about two and a half hours after the collision, the last distress rocket had been fired in vain and the last lifeboat was lowered. Minutes later a huge wave swept over the boat deck. The gigantic liner slowly tilted forward as her bow went down. Deck chairs, loose rigging, screaming passengers slid in crashing confusion down the sloping decks. As the angle steepened, the ship's tremendous screws rose out of water. With a screeching of steel the forward funnel tore loose and plummeted into the sea. A thunderous rumble followed as the liner's gigantic engines sheared from their beds and crashed toward the bow through bulkhead after bulkhead. The *Titanic's* stern climbed high out of water, paused, then plunged beneath the cold waters of the North Atlantic, silencing the anguished moans of those who still clung to her.

In seconds one of nature's simplest creations—a block of frozen water—had destroyed a monument to maritime safety: the "unsinkable ship." The price for flouting nature with one of man's creations was the loss of 1,517 lives.

The painful memory of the *Titanic* was still fresh in the public's mind in the spring of 1915, when another British superliner sank under circumstances that were to help lead the United States into World War I.

On February 18, 1915, Germany had ordered a submarine blockade of the British Isles in reply to the British declaration that it would blockade enemy coasts. On May 1 one of the largest and most luxurious liners afloat, the *Lusitania,* set sail from New York to Europe via the British Isles. Shortly before she left, the German Embassy placed a warning in New York newspapers that all vessels flying the flag of Great Britain or her allies were liable to destruction in British waters and that travelers sailing in the war zone did so at their own risk. No one took the warning seriously. The 32,000-ton British Cunard liner left on schedule under the command of Captain W. H. Turner, with a crew of over 600 and 1,253 passengers, among them 179 Americans. Her cargo consisted of copper articles, brass, furs, and small-arms ammunition, but no high explosives or loaded shells.

TEXT CONTINUED ON PAGE 166

The Titanic (*opposite, above*) was commanded by the veteran White Star captain Edward J. Smith (*opposite, below*) on her ill-fated maiden voyage from Southampton to New York. When the "unsinkable" liner struck an iceberg and went down, 1,517 of the 2,224 people aboard were lost. The above picture of survivors was taken from the Carpathia. *The total capacity of the Titanic's lifeboats (some of them at left) was only 1,178.* OVERLEAF: *Crowds await news outside the White Star Line offices on Broadway in New York City.*

As the unarmed liner approached the coast of Ireland, the British Admiralty advised Captain Turner by wireless to take precautions because of German submarine activity in the area. The captain posted extra watches and had the lifeboats swung out on their davits, but he did not steer the evasive zigzag course suggested by the Admiralty. The British sent no military vessel to accompany the *Lusitania* in the belief that an escort might invite attack.

Shortly after 2:00 P.M. on the afternoon of May 7, the ship was ten miles off Old Head of Kinsale, a cape on the southwestern coast of Ireland, when a lookout sighted the wake of a torpedo streaking toward the starboard bow. There was no time to avoid it, and the explosion rocked the ship, showering passengers at luncheon with flying debris. Shocked and surprised, but without undue panic, they immediately began to make their way toward the boat deck as the *Lusitania* listed to starboard. A second, more violent explosion quickly followed the first. Many thought that the ship had been struck by another torpedo, but this was later believed to have been one of the boilers exploding. The ship was still moving forward at about seventeen knots, and it was impossible to reduce her speed because the steam lines had been severed and there was no steam to reverse her turbine engines. Captain Turner set a course for shore. The SOS that he ordered sent out was received at Queenstown at 2:15 P.M., and the Naval station there quickly dispatched the tugs *Warrior, Stormcock,* and *Julia,* together with five trawlers and a tug towing a lifeboat. It would take the rescuers two hours to reach the scene.

Meanwhile the *Lusitania* was about to sink. She had listed so rapidly to starboard that only two of her port lifeboats had been able to get away. Yet despite the awkward tilt, many passengers still thought that she was unsinkable, that her watertight compartments would hold. Some of the lifeboats that were launched were swamped in the vortex of the fast-foundering ship. People began dropping into the sea from ropes that had been hung over the sides. Some hundred passengers clung to the high port side until the *Lusitania* began to settle by her bow. Then when her broad stern lurched up into the air and the sunlight glinted momentarily on her four polished bronze propellers, all one hundred cascaded down the deck. Eighteen minutes after she was torpedoed, the ship slid beneath the sea with steam hissing from her four funnels. The death toll was 1,198, including 128 Americans. (One was Alfred G. Vanderbilt, who was last seen giving his life belt to a woman passenger who had none.)

The unwarranted attack on the defenseless *Lusitania* was largely responsible for shifting much of the pro-German feeling in the United States to the side of Britain and her allies. President Woodrow Wilson sent a severe note of protest to Berlin, demanding an apology, reparations, and assurances that no such incident would ever happen again. Germany agreed not to attack liners without warning, but on February 10, 1916, she announced that armed merchant ships would be considered warships and sunk without warning. Wilson retorted that international law permitted commercial ships to be armed for self-defense. In the early months of 1917, however, Germany began unrestricted submarine warfare on all vessels. On April 6 the United States declared war on Germany.

*   *   *

Eight days outbound from her home port of Genoa, Italy, the plush 29,100-ton Italian liner *Andrea Doria* sliced through the gentle North Atlantic swells south of Nantucket on a foggy night in July, 1956. She was to dock in New York the next day, and some of the 1,706 passengers had gone below to finish packing. Others strolled the deck in the thickening mist, listening to the sentimental strains of "Arrivederci, Roma" that drifted out of the Belvedere lounge, where an orchestra played for late-night dancers. Card-room bridge games were drawing to a close, and at the bars, shipboard acquaintances were drinking farewell toasts. It was a typical last night aboard the three-year-old *Andrea Doria,* the veteran of 101 transatlantic crossings.

Not many miles away the 12,644-ton Swedish-American liner *Stockholm* was spending her first night at sea en route from New York to Copenhagen. She was heading east along the edge of the northern route in the heavily traveled shipping lanes south of Nantucket known as the Times Square of the North Atlantic. Although it is not obligatory, it is customary in this congested area of the ocean for eastbound traffic to take the southern sea lane and westbound traffic to take the northern sea lane.

TEXT CONTINUED ON PAGE 172

Before the British Cunarder Lusitania *made her fatal trip from*
New York to Europe in 1915,
the German Embassy in Wash-
ington inserted the warning at
left in New York papers. Struck
by two German torpedoes off the
Irish coast, the liner sank so
quickly that 1,198 lives were lost.
Opposite, top, is an artist's ren-
dition of the tragedy, and below
it the announcement in The
New York Times. *X's super-*
imposed on a photo of the Lusitania *mark the spots where the*
enemy torpedoes hit the ship.

OCEAN STEAMSHIPS.
CUNARD

EUROPE VIA LIVERPOOL
LUSITANIA
Fastest and Largest Steamer
now in Atlantic Service Sails
SATURDAY, MAY 1, 10 A.M.
Transylvania, Fri., May 7, 5 P.M.
Orduna, - - Tues., May 18, 10 A.M.
Tuscania, - - Fri., May 21, 5 P.M.
LUSITANIA, Sat., May 29, 10 A.M.
Transylvania, Fri., June 4, 5 P.M.

Gibraltar—Genoa—Naples—Piraeus
S.S. Carpathia, Thur., May 13, Noon

NOTICE!
TRAVELLERS intending to
embark on the Atlantic voyage
are reminded that a state of
war exists between Germany
and her allies and Great Britain
and her allies; that the zone of
war includes the waters adjacent to the British Isles; that,
in accordance with formal notice given by the Imperial German Government, vessels flying
the flag of Great Britain, or of
any of her allies, are liable to
destruction in those waters and
that travellers sailing in the
war zone on ships of Great
Britain or her allies do so at
their own risk.

IMPERIAL GERMAN EMBASSY
WASHINGTON, D. C., APRIL 22, 1915.

OVERLEAF: *The Italian liner*
Andrea Doria *settles before*
sinking in the Atlantic off Nan-
tucket in July, 1956. During the
previous night she had been
struck in the starboard side by the
Swedish-American liner Stockholm. *Fortunately, help came*
quickly and the Andrea Doria
was slow to go down. When she
finally disappeared beneath the
waves, nearly eleven hours after
the collision, 1,656 people had
been saved and 50 had been lost.

LUSITANIA SUNK BY A SUBMARINE, PROBABLY 1,000 DEAD;
TWICE TORPEDOED OFF IRISH COAST; SINKS IN 15 MINUTES;
AMERICANS ABOARD INCLUDED VANDERBILT AND FROHMAN;
WASHINGTON BELIEVES THAT A GRAVE CRISIS IS AT HAND

In clear weather the *Stockholm*'s course would not have been a hazardous one. But for three days fog had blanketed the sea from the Newfoundland Banks to Nantucket, and the limit of visibility was now not much farther than from the bridge to the bow. Like most ships on a tight schedule, the *Stockholm* slackened speed only slightly for the fog, the captain relying on his radar to scan the invisible sea ahead.

At 11:20 P.M. a passenger aboard the *Andrea Doria* was surprised to see lights looming out of the fog. Almost before he realized what they were, there was a shuddering crash and the *Stockholm*'s reinforced prow knifed thirty feet into the *Andrea Doria*'s starboard side. For an instant the two ships clung together; then with a flurry of sparks and a shrieking of ruptured steel, they fell apart.

In that brief moment the gay, peaceful world of the *Andrea Doria* became a nightmare of death and confusion. On her decks, strolling passengers were slammed into ventilators and bulkheads. In the Belvedere lounge, dancers were knocked into a jumbled heap on the floor. In the card rooms, tables were jerked from their fastenings, while at the bars, drinkers were showered with broken glass. Below decks, passengers were lifted from their beds and hurled against cabin walls. One man had been brushing his teeth when the collision occurred. When he looked back to where his wife had been reading in bed, there was only a gaping hole in the side of the ship. His wife and the bed were gone. Incredibly, a fourteen-year-old girl was snatched from her cabin on the *Andrea Doria* by the *Stockholm*'s prow and later found unconscious but unharmed amid the twisted steel bow plates of the Swedish-American liner.

Smoke and dust drifted through passageways. As the *Andrea Doria* started to settle on her starboard side, water and oil sloshed through the corridors. Over the ship's loudspeakers officers asked everyone to remain calm, but the orders were in Italian and many people did not hear or could not understand them.

Two minutes after the collision, the *Andrea Doria*'s radio operator sent off an urgent request for help: *SOS . . . collision . . . 40° 30'N, 60° 53'W . . . Send immediate assistance.* The same signals were being sent from the *Stockholm*.

After the initial panic, passengers on the Italian liner made their way through the baggage-cluttered passageways to the boat deck. Although the ship's lights flickered, they remained on, helping to quell much of the confusion. As the ship slowly settled from a 25-degree to a 35-degree list, eight lifeboats full of people managed to get away from the low starboard side. The port side was too high in the water for the boats to be lowered. Then the ship tilted to a 45-degree angle, and those who clung to her steep decks prayed that help would arrive in time.

From out of the fog came lifeboats from the *Stockholm*, whose crew had managed to seal off the damage to the Swedish liner's prow, allowing her captain to bring her about to help in the rescue. Meanwhile, other ships raced to the aid of the *Andrea Doria*. The seven-thousand-ton freighter *Cape Ann* was fifty-five minutes away; the destroyer escort *Edward H. Allen* was fifty-two miles distant; the military transport *Private William H. Thomas* was twenty miles off; the majestic old *Ile de France*, outward bound for Europe, had turned and was heading for the stricken Italian liner at twenty-two knots.

Two hours later the French ship appeared, with all her lights blazing to cheer the survivors. Her ten lifeboats joined others that were taking off the *Andrea Doria*'s passengers.

By dawn the fog had lifted and the only people aboard the Italian ship were her captain and a score of crewmen still trying to level her with auxiliary pumps. Finally, at 7:00 A.M. they realized the hopelessness of their task and allowed themselves to be taken off. The liner lingered on until at 10:00 A.M., eleven hours after the collision, she slowly rolled over on her beam-ends, and in a welter of bubbles, sank bow first in 225 feet of water. Although the tragedy cost the lives of fifty people, 1,656 were saved. And no small tribute was due to the *Andrea Doria*, a mortally wounded ship that was slow to die.

This buoy marked the grave of the submarine Thresher, *which sank off New England.*

CHAPTER THIRTEEN

The Mystery
of the
Deadly Bermuda
Triangle

On May 21, 1968, the nuclear-powered United States submarine *Scorpion*, homeward bound from maneuvers in the Mediterranean, surfaced about midnight in the North Atlantic some 250 miles west of the Azores to send a routine radio message to her base at Norfolk, Virginia. After reporting her position, westward course, and estimated time of arrival, the *Scorpion* and her ninety-nine-man crew returned to the silent depths. No one ever saw the submarine or her men again.

When she failed to appear off the Virginia coast, the Navy issued an ominous bulletin: the *Scorpion* was two days overdue; repeated attempts to establish radio contact with her had been unsuccessful. A massive air and sea search was initiated, but finally, on June 5, the *Scorpion* and her crew were listed as "presumed lost." For months no debris, no oil slick, no trace of the submarine was found. Then, on October 30, a Naval oceanographic research ship, the *Mizar*, towing a sensitive metal detector and deep-sea cameras twenty-five feet above

The "Bermuda Triangle" is an area of ocean roughly limited by Bermuda, Puerto Rico, and the coast of Florida. In and around it more than forty ships and twenty airplanes have simply disappeared within the past century. Among them were the nuclear-powered U.S. submarine Scorpion (above), which vanished in 1968 while homeward bound from the Mediterranean, and the U.S. Navy supply ship Cyclops (below), which disappeared in 1918 somewhere between Barbados, W. I., and Virginia.

the bottom, found and photographed what was believed to be the shattered remains of the *Scorpion*'s hull four hundred miles southwest of the Azores at a depth of more than ten thousand feet. No one knows for certain what happened to the submarine, but wherever old seamen gather to talk, many blame its disappearance on the "Deadly Bermuda Triangle," a term first popularized by Vincent Gaddis writing in *Argosy* magazine in 1964.

The Bermuda Triangle is an area of ocean in which more than forty ships and twenty airplanes have vanished without a trace over the past hundred years. To visualize it, draw a line from Bermuda to Florida, another from Bermuda to Puerto Rico, and a third line from Puerto Rico through the Bahamas back to Florida. Actually, this is only the center of the area in which disappearances have occurred. Other mysteries have taken place in adjacent areas to the north and east in the Atlantic, south in the Caribbean, and west in the Gulf of Mexico. When all these disappearances are plotted on a globe, the "triangle" becomes more of a square, its north and south boundaries being 20° and 30° north latitude and its east and west boundaries being the east coast of the United States and 60° west longitude. When the airplanes and ships vanished in this area there were no notable marine or meteorological disturbances; they issued no distress calls, and with only two exceptions, no wreckage, survivors, or bodies were ever found. Here are a few case histories that have given the Bermuda Triangle its sinister reputation.

On January 31, 1880, the British frigate *Atlanta,* a sturdy training vessel with 290 cadets and crewmen aboard, sailed from Bermuda bound for England. The weather was clear; the seas moderate. Yet the *Atlanta* vanished without leaving so much as a broken spar behind.

On March 4, 1918, the 19,000-ton Navy supply ship U.S.S. *Cyclops* left Barbados, in the West Indies, for Norfolk, Virginia. The 500-foot ship carried 309 passengers and a valuable cargo of 10,800 tons of manganese ore. The weather was fair. No radio messages were received. When it became clear that the *Cyclops* was overdue, an intensive search was launched. Months later the Navy summed up its investigation with this statement: "The disappearance of this ship has been one of the most baffling mysteries in the annals of the Navy, all attempts to locate her having proved unsuccessful. Many theories have been advanced, but none that satisfactorily accounts for her disappearance."

In 1925 the cargo ship S.S. *Cotopaxi,* out of Charleston, North Carolina, vanished just as inexplicably on a voyage to Havana. The following year the freighter *Suduffco,* sailing south from Port Newark with a crew of twenty-nine, also disappeared in the Bermuda Triangle.

In June, 1950, the 350-foot freighter *Sandra* left Savannah, Georgia, for Puerto Cabello, Venezuela, carrying 300 tons of insecticide. She was known to have passed Jacksonville, then St. Augustine, Florida, in the calm semitropical night. Then she vanished without a trace.

On February 2, 1963, the 554-foot tanker *Marine Sulphur Queen* left Beaumont, Texas, for Norfolk, Virginia. She carried a crew of thirty-nine and a cargo of molten sulfur in heavily insulated steel tanks. The sulfur was kept at a temperature of 265 degrees by special heating coils, and was said to be no more dangerous than any other cargo.

On the night of February 3, a routine radio message from the tanker placed her off the Dry Tortugas due west of Key West, Florida. This was the last anyone heard from the vessel. When she was reported overdue on February 6, planes and Coast Guard cutters from Norfolk to Key West scoured the area. One plane spotted a "yellow substance" on the surface of the sea 240 miles southeast of Jacksonville, but it proved to be a patch of drifting seaweed. On February 14, five days after the search was abandoned, a Navy plane, flying over the Florida Straits, sighted some debris, and a life jacket that was thought to have come from the *Marine Sulphur Queen.* Nothing else was ever found.

When a vessel the size of a steamer or a tanker goes down, many objects usually float free, and a telltale oil slick bubbles to the surface sometimes for years to mark the spot where the ship sank. Yet in the Bermuda Triangle such evidence has never appeared. Most puzzling of all, why have the ships, sailing in calm weather, and equipped with adequate marine radios, failed to get off at least one distress call before catastrophe struck?

Even stranger are the circumstances surrounding the disappearance of aircraft flying over the Bermuda Triangle. The first incident occurred on December 5, 1945, only a few months after the end of World War II. Five TBM Avenger bombers took off from the United States Naval Air Station at Fort Lauderdale, Florida, for a routine patrol. The weather was clear; the sea calm. The propeller-driven aircraft carried capacity fuel loads and a total of fourteen veteran crewmen. Standard flight procedure called for them to fly a triangular course out over the empty ocean: 160 miles due east, then 40 miles due north, then back southwest directly to Fort Lauderdale again. The Naval Air Station regularly dispatched such patrols as part of our Coastal Defense System.

The planes left the field at 2:30 P.M. and headed east in formation over the Atlantic at 215 miles per hour. They were not expected to contact the ground until 3:45 P.M., when the flight leader would call the tower for landing instructions. The call came as expected, but it was far from routine.

"Calling tower . . . this is an emergency . . . this is an emergency!" There was a worried note in the flight leader's voice.

The tower gave him clearance and awaited his reply. After a long pause the pilot said, "We cannot see land . . . repeat . . . we cannot see land!"

"What is your position?" the tower radioed back.

"We're not sure of our position," came the reply. "We can't be sure where we are . . . we seem to be lost."

Startled tower personnel stared at each other in disbelief. How could experienced pilots and navigators of five planes become lost under such ideal flying conditions?

"Assume bearing due west," the tower instructed. The reply was even more incredible.

"We don't know which way is west," said the alarmed flight leader. "Everything is wrong . . . strange. We can't be sure of any direction. Even the ocean doesn't look as it should."

At that moment the sun was approaching the western horizon. Even if all five planes' compasses had failed, why couldn't the men take their bearings on the sun?

During the next forty minutes, the control tower heard the bomber crews talking among themselves. The planes were obviously within sight of each other, but the conversations were filled with growing fear.

For no other possible reason than doubt and panic, the flight leader suddenly turned his command over to another plane. This in itself indicated that the patrol was in an extremely desperate situation.

At 4:25 P.M. the flight leader contacted the tower. "We are not certain where we are," he said. "We think we must be about two hundred and twenty-five miles northeast of base . . . looks like we are—" The message broke off abruptly.

Immediately a Martin Mariner flying boat with full rescue equipment and a thirteen-man crew was dispatched toward the area. Meanwhile, the tower repeatedly tried to reach the missing aircraft on the radio to tell them that help was on the way. There was no answer.

At first, routine reports came in from the flying boat. But twenty minutes after it took off, when the tower tried to contact it for a position report, there was no answer.

The air base immediately notified the Miami Coast Guard and sent a call for help to Naval Headquarters. Shortly after dusk, a Coast Guard rescue plane flying the same course as the flying boat reached the last estimated position of the missing patrol. Navy and Coast Guard surface craft soon joined the search. All that night powerful searchlights probed the black Atlantic and found nothing. There were no signal flares, no life rafts, no wreckage, no survivors.

At dawn the escort carrier *Solomons* added its thirty planes to the search. By midafternoon twenty-one Navy and Coast Guard vessels were scouring the sea, while overhead three hundred airplanes flew a grid search pattern. From nearby territorial islands, the British Royal Air Force threw every available aircraft into the ever-widening search, which extended from Florida to the Bahamas and two hundred miles into the Gulf of Mexico.

Twelve large land parties carefully searched three hundred miles of shoreline from St. Augustine to Miami Beach. They found nothing. Six airplanes and twenty-seven men had simply vanished.

Military authorities were completely baffled. Had the planes wandered aimlessly over the ocean until they were forced down for lack of fuel? If this were the case, the Avengers, although not particularly buoyant, would have remained afloat at least long enough for the airmen to inflate the life rafts and Mae West life jackets with which all the planes were equipped. In similar ditchings, airmen had survived in the open ocean for weeks. If the Mariner flying boat also went down, it would have remained afloat much longer than the Avengers. Why had not one plane out of the six (including the Mariner) gotten off a single SOS? Each aircraft had a radio; the Mariner even had a hand-crank generator in case the electrical system failed.

There seemed to be no logical answers to these questions. "They vanished as completely," said an officer on the Naval Board of Inquiry, "as if they had flown to Mars." After its exhaustive study of all the known facts, the board summed up the strange incident with this statement: "We are not able to even make a good guess as to what happened."

This was only the beginning of unusual aircraft disappearances in the Bermuda Triangle. On January 29, 1948, the British South American Airways four-engine airliner the *Star Tiger* was en route to Kingston, Jamaica, when it radioed the following message to Bermuda at 10:30 P.M.: "We are on course four hundred miles from Bermuda tower. Weather excellent and the ship performing well. We should arrive Jamaica on schedule."

But the *Star Tiger* and its passengers were never heard from again.

On December 28, 1948, a DC-3 passenger plane flying from San Juan, Puerto Rico, to Florida—a distance of only one thousand miles—had almost reached its destination when something happened. Within sight of the lights of Miami, the pilot sent his last radio report at 4:13 A.M. "We're approaching the field. Only fifty miles out to the south. All's well. Will stand by for landing instructions." Then the plane vanished.

Less than a month later, on January 17, 1949, the *Ariel,* owned by the same company and bound for the same destination as its ill-fated sister ship, the *Star Tiger,* disappeared under similarly strange circumstances. Carrying thirteen passengers and a crew of seven, the four-engine airliner refueled at Bermuda and took off at 7:30 A.M. on a perfectly clear day. Fifty-five minutes later, the pilot radioed a routine flight report to Bermuda.

"This is Captain McPhee aboard the *Ariel* en route to Kingston, Jamaica, from Bermuda. We have reached cruising altitude. Fair weather. Expected time of arrival Kingston as scheduled."

There were no further reports, no wreckage, no survivors, no clues.

Periodically over the years there have been other mystifying accidents. On January 8, 1962, a KB-50 Air Force tanker left Langley Air Force Base, Virginia, on a flight to the Azores. Shortly afterward, the Langley tower received a weak radio message saying that the aircraft was in some kind of trouble; then the garbled signals lapsed into silence. Neither the plane nor its crew were ever found.

On August 28, 1963, two KC-135 four-engine Strato-tanker jets took off from Homestead Air Force Base, Florida, on a refueling mission over the Atlantic. At noon the jets radioed their position as eight hundred miles northwest of Miami and three hundred miles west of Bermuda. Then they disappeared.

An Air Force statement said that "the planes were not flying close together." But when debris was found floating on the water some 260 miles southwest of Bermuda, searchers suspected a midair collision. Then, two days later, more debris turned up—but it was found 160 miles from where the first was discovered. No one knows what happened.

What possible explanations can there be for these sudden accidents? There are indications that some powerful and as yet unknown physical force is at work in the Bermuda Triangle. Experts who have studied all the evidence have ruled out such known hazards as sudden tropical storms and waterspouts. They speculate instead about such possibilities as atmospheric aberrations and electromagnetic gravitational disturbances—broad, impressive terms that could mean any number of unknown abnormal conditions that might occur in the air or in the earth's magnetic field. In his book *Invisible Horizons,* Vincent Gaddis says that after his Bermuda Triangle article appeared in *Argosy,* he received a number of letters from readers suggesting causes of the strange disappearances. Explanations ranged all the way from flying saucers to "disintegrating rays from a 30,000-year-old Atlantean power plant." Gaddis speculated that in the case of the missing Avengers, something had affected their compasses and may have silenced their radios. When the Mariner rescue plane flew into the same zone, it too was affected. Combining these factors with the strange appearance of the sea and the inability of the pilots to see the sun, he suggested the theory of an atmospheric aberration—a phenomenon that Gaddis said "might be called 'a hole in the sky.'" This metaphor refers to an area of unknown origin that airplanes can enter but cannot leave.

Gaddis added that officially the Navy did not go along with his theory.

Captain E. W. Humphrey, coordinator of aviation safety, said: "It is not felt that an atmospheric aberration exists in this area, nor that one has existed in the past. Fleet aircraft and patrol flights are conducted regularly in this same area without incident."

Indeed, the Bermuda Triangle is far from being an isolated area. It is crisscrossed daily by many planes and ships—both military and civilian—without mishap. But considering that in this same area there is an abnormal number of totally inexplicable disappearances, then there is room to believe that a factor greater than chance may be involved in these mysterious accidents. Whether it is called an atmospheric aberration or something else, it strikes without warning frequently enough to be alarming.

Dick Stern, one of Gaddis' readers from Atlanta, Georgia, wrote of two experiences he had had that tend to support the theory of atmospheric aberration. He said that during the last two weeks of 1944 his bombing group had left the United States to replace war-battered groups in Italy. His plane was not more than three hundred miles from Bermuda on a beautiful clear night when "we were suddenly whipped over on our backs, found ourselves on the ceiling one moment and pinned down the next, as the ship was thrown about at an incredible rate of speed." By the time the pilot and copilot pulled the bomber out of its dive, the prop wash was creating whitecaps on the water below.

The incident so shook the airmen that they turned the plane back to Bermuda. There Stern found that of the seven bombers that had started out in his group, only two had returned. Nothing was ever heard of the others and no wreckage was ever found despite a thorough search.

In 1961 Stern and his wife were flying from London to Miami aboard a commercial airliner that stopped at Bermuda and Nassau. Shortly after the Bristol Britannia took off from Bermuda on a clear day with only a distant thunderstorm on the horizon, Stern was relating his near-fatal Air Force experience to his wife and to the pilot when the plane suddenly dropped with such force that "the food we were eating was thrown to the ceiling. Fortunately we had our seat belts fastened or we would have hit the ceiling in the same manner," said Stern. "After a harrowing fifteen minutes of up and down, and no storm in our immediate vicinity, we managed to clear the area."

This kind of turbulence could explain some but not all of the aircraft losses in the Bermuda Triangle. One theory is that a combination of destructive forces are involved—atmospheric aberrations that may cause magnetic and possibly gravitational disturbances severe enough to disintegrate both planes and ships.

In August, 1968, Ivan T. Sanderson wrote an article in *Argosy* entitled "The Spreading Mystery of the Bermuda Triangle." He found that when he plotted the locations of ship, plane, and submarine disasters, the majority of *complete disappearances* had taken place in six distinct lozenge-shaped areas around the world. Oddly enough, all six areas were approximately the same size and shape and were located in the same latitudes north and south of the equator. Three fell between 30° and 40° north latitude, and three between 30° and 40° south latitude. Those north of the equator include the Bermuda Triangle; the Mediterranean Sea, where French and Israeli submarines have vanished as recently as January, 1968; and the "Devil's Sea" region of the Pacific, just south of Japan. Those south of the equator lie off the southeast coasts of South America, South Africa, and Australia. What is particularly interesting about five of these strikingly similar areas (excluding the Mediterranean) is that they all lie on the right, or east, sides of continents *precisely* in the latitudes where warm surface currents sweep northward to collide with cold southbound currents. "These are the areas of extreme temperature variabilities which alone would predict a very high incidence of violent marine and aerial disturbances," said Sanderson. "What more likely areas for storms and wrecks and founderings and even magnetic anomalies?"

The graveyards of the Atlantic at Cape Hatteras and Sable Island are two inshore examples of what nature's conflicting forces can do. But beyond the shoals, in the open ocean, who can say what may occur under certain ideal conditions when contrary currents, temperature inversions, atmospheric aberrations, and other less known forces combine?

Assuming that something of this nature is occurring, why then is there seldom, if ever, any trace of debris after the ships or submarines or aircraft have been destroyed? The lesson of the *Thresher* is instructive.

On April 10, 1963, the nuclear-powered United States submarine *Thresher* disappeared mysteriously off the New England coast while on a test dive. Her last, badly garbled radio message was thought to have contained the words "test depth," the submarine's lowest diving limit.

Every resource of the United States Navy was thrown into the search that followed. Sonar scanned the bottom for questionable "bumps" that might be the *Thresher*. Ships scanned the surface for oil slicks and debris, while their sensitive instruments listened around the clock for any unusual noises underwater. But the *Thresher* and her compliment of 129 men had simply vanished.

Temporarily, there the matter rested. It was another enigma for the record book, another unexplained mystery.

Then, four months later, part of the mystery was solved with the use of a deep-water submersible, one of the few vessels capable of approaching the ocean's extreme depths. After repeated dives, the Navy bathyscaph *Trieste* found the remains of the *Thresher* in 8,400 feet of water. The 300-foot-long submarine had imploded from water pressures of up to two tons per square inch. As a result, thousands of pieces of torn twisted metal littered the bottom as far as the bathyscaph's crew could see. According to Lieutenant Commander Donald L. Keach, the area looked like a "vast junkyard."

No one knows positively what caused the *Thresher* to sink, but the wreckage shows what can happen to a steel vessel 8,400 feet down.

It so happens that far greater depths occur in the six lozenge-shaped areas where the greatest number of air and sea craft have vanished without a trace. In the northern hemisphere, the Hatteras Abyssal Plain under the Bermuda Triangle is 20,994 feet deep; the Ionian Basin beneath the Mediterranean Sea is 16,896 feet deep; the Philippean Abyssal Plain under the Devil's Sea is 21,596 feet deep. In the southern hemisphere, the Southeast Australian Abyssal Plain off the coast of Australia is 17,278 feet deep; the Madagascar Abyssal Plain off Africa is 18,827 feet deep; and the Argentine Abyssal Plain off South America is 19,736 feet deep. In other words, anything that sank in these waters would have to fall from 3.01 to 4.09 miles before reaching bottom. No one knows where abyssal currents might carry shattered wreckage, but in those depths the debris would be inaccessible to our most advanced underwater salvage vessels.

The Gulf Stream skirts the western edge of the Hatteras Abyssal

TEXT CONTINUED ON PAGE 188

The nuclear-powered U.S. Navy submarine Thresher *vanished during a test dive on*

April 10, 1963. Four months later the remains were found in 8,400 feet of water.

Plain in the Bermuda Triangle, and it could have a great deal to do with the lack of wreckage in some of the mysterious sinkings. In July, 1969, when Swiss oceanographic engineer Jacques Piccard and five others aboard the research submersible *Ben Franklin* drifted submerged in the Stream for almost 1,500 miles, Piccard noted these peculiarities: "The Gulf Stream, the surging river that rushes out of the Gulf of Mexico . . . is not merely one flood of water but several swirling, colliding, meandering torrents tumbling northward . . . it has internal waves of wide amplitude, sixty, sometimes one hundred or more feet. . . . When we are in them, we go up and down the Stream. . . ." The *Ben Franklin* did not drift ashore but was swept northward at depths from six hundred to two thousand feet until the seven-hundred-ton vessel was ejected from the stream near the Graveyard of the Atlantic at Cape Hatteras.

Under these circumstances it is no wonder that wreckage is seldom found at the scene of an accident after a ship or plane has gone down in the Gulf Stream.

Whatever causes the strange accidents in the Bermuda Triangle and the five other "vicious vortexes" of the world may not be a secret for long. Scientists and technicians are building progressively better deep-sea submersibles to plumb the oceans' mysteries. The government recently announced that it is marshaling the technical know-how and sophisticated electronic equipment of four government agencies[1] to develop a device that will warn pilots of an atmospheric aberration technically known as Clear-Air Turbulence, or CAT, that has been blamed for the inflight destruction of some aircraft. The Navy is currently investigating electromagnetic gravitational disturbances with a classified program called Project Magnet.

Once we have the results of these programs, once we know more about abyssal depths, atmospheric aberrations, and magnetic anomalies, then we may have the key to one of the greatest mysteries of all time— the secret of the Deadly Bermuda Triangle.

---

[1] Department of Commerce Environmental Science Services Administration (ESSA); Department of Defense; Department of Transportation; and the National Aeronautics and Space Administration (NASA).

Appendix ❧❧❧

A Chronology of Marine Disasters from The Encyclopedia Americana

1831, July 19 — Immigrant vessel *Lady Sherbrooke*, bound from England to Quebec, wrecked off Cape Ray; 263 die.

1833, May 11 — Ship *Lady of the Lake*, sailing from England to Quebec, hit by iceberg; 215 die.

1847, April 29 — Immigrant ship *Exmouth* bound for Quebec from Londonderry, lost; 200 lost.

1850, March 29 — Steamer *Royal Adelaide* wrecked off Margate, England; 400 lost.

1852, March 26 — Troopship *Birkenhead*, bound from Queenstown, South Africa, to Cape of Good Hope wrecked; 454 lost.

1853, Sept. 29 — Immigrant vessel *Annie Jane* wrecked off Scotland; 348 die.

1854, March — *City of Glasgow*, bound for Philadelphia from Liverpool, vanishes with 450 aboard.

1854, Sept. 27 — The *Arctic* sinks in collision near Grand Banks, Newfoundland; 322 lost.

1857, Sept. 12 — Steamer *Central America* sinks in gale en route to New York City from Havana; about 400 lost.

1858, Sept. 13 — The *Austria*, a steamer headed for New York City from Hamburg; catches fire; 471 die.

1859, April 27 — The *Pomona* is wrecked off Ireland en route to New York City from Liverpool; 386 lives lost.

1859, Oct. 25 — The *Royal Charter* is wrecked and about 450 lives lost in Irish Sea off coast of Anglesea.

1860, Sept. 8 — Lake Michigan excursion steamer *Lady Elgin* collides with lumber ship; 300 dead.

1865, April 27 — River steamer *Sultana* explodes near Memphis, Tenn., and sinks; 1,450 dead.

1867, Oct. 29 — Mail boats *Rhone* and *Wye* and many small vessels wrecked in storm at St. Thomas, West Indies; about 1,000 lost.

1870, Sept. 17 — British warship *Captain* founders off Finistère in France; 472 die.

1873, April 1 — British steamer *Atlantic* is wrecked off Nova Scotia; 547 aboard die.

1878, Sept. 3 — English steamer *Princess Alice* sinks after collision in Thames; 700 persons killed.

1890, Sept. 19 — Turkish frigate *Ertogrul* burns off Japanese coast; about 540 lost.

1891, March 17 — British steamer *Utopia* sinks in collision off Gibraltar; 574 die.

1898, Feb. 15 — U. S. battleship *Maine* blows up in harbor at Havana, Cuba; 264 killed.

1898, July 4 — 560 lives lost in collision of French liner *La Bourgogne* and British *Cromartyshire* near Sable Island, off Nova Scotia.

1904, June 15 — Steamboat *General Slocum* burns in New York City's East River; more than 1,000 perish.

1904, June 28 — Some 600 die in wreck of *Norge* on Rockall Reef, off Scotland.

1912, March 5 — Spanish steamer *Principe de Asturias* wrecked on rocks off northern coast; about 500 drowned.

1912, April 15 — Liner *Titanic* strikes iceberg in North Atlantic on maiden voyage from Southampton to New York City; toll variously estimated at 1,490, 1,502, and 1,517.

1912, Sept. 28 — Japanese steamer *Kichemaru* sinks off coast of Japan; about 1,000 lost.

1914, May 29 — Canadian Pacific liner *Empress of Ireland* sinks after collision with Norwegian collier in St. Lawrence River; lost 1,024.

1915, May 7 — British passenger liner *Lusitania* sunk by German submarine in Atlantic Ocean off southwestern coast of Ireland; 1,195 (or 1,198) dead, including about 124 Americans.

1915, June 24 — Excursion steamer *Eastland* explodes in Chicago River, Illinois; more than 800 die.

1916, Aug. 29 — Estimated 1,000 perish in sinking of *Hsin Yu* off coast of China.

1917, July 9 — British warship *Vanguard* blows up at Scapa Flow dock; about 800 killed.

1919, Jan. 17 — Wreck of French steamer *Chaonia* in Strait of Messina kills 460.

1921, March 18 — Steamer *Hongkong* wrecked on rocks off Swatow, China; estimated 1,000 dead.

1926, Oct. 16 — Chinese troopship explodes in Yangtze River, killing estimated 1,200.

1927, Oct. 25 — About 326 perish in sinking of Italian ship *Principessa Mafalda* after explosion off Pôrto Segura, Bahia, Brazil.

1928, Nov. 12 — British steamship *Vestris* founders off the Virginia capes; 113 lost.

1931, June 14 — French excursion steamer overturns in gale off St.-Nazaire; approximately 450 lost.

1934, Sept. 8 — S. S. *Morro Castle* burns off coast of New Jersey and is beached at Asbury Park; 137 dead.

1942, Oct. 2 — *Queen Mary* rams and sinks British cruiser *Curaçao* off English coast; 338 on cruiser die.

1942, Oct. 26 — More than 200 Jewish refugees from Bulgaria drown in shipwreck in Sea of Marmara.

1944, Dec. 17–18 — Typhoon strikes task force of U. S. Third Fleet in Philippine Sea; almost 800 officers and men lost; 3 destroyers capsized, 6 or 7 other ships seriously damaged; 146 aircraft destroyed.

1945, April 9 — United States Liberty ship explodes in harbor at Bari, Italy; 360 dead, 1,730 injured.

1946, Aug. 2 — Steamer *Vitya* sinks in Lake Nyasa, Tanganyika; 295 drowned.

1947, Jan. 19 — Greek steamer *Himara* strikes mine off Athens, sinks in 30 minutes; at least 392 die.

1948, Jan. 28 — Freighter *Joo Maru* strikes mine and sinks in Japan's Inland Sea; 250 lost.

1948, Feb. 28 — Steamer capsizes during pirate attack near Amoy, China; 160 die.

1948, June 11 — Danish passenger ship *Kjoebenhavn* sinks after striking mine off coast of Jutland; at least 140 die.

1948, Dec. 3 — Chinese steamer explodes and sinks south of Shanghai; 1,100 missing or dead.

1949, Jan. 27 – Chinese liner and collier collide and sink off coast of southern China; at least 600 dead.

1949, Sept. 17 – Great Lakes passenger ship *Noronic* burns at pier in Toronto, Canada, killing about 130 and injuring more than 100.

1950, Jan. 12 – British submarine *Truculent* rammed by Swedish tanker in Thames estuary; 65 dead.

1951, April 16 – British submarine *Affray* sunk off the Isle of Wight; 75 lost.

1952, April 26 – United States destroyer-minesweeper *Hobson* sinks after colliding with aircraft carrier *Wasp* during Atlantic maneuvers; 176 lost.

1953, Jan. 31 – Ferry sinks in storm off Donaghadee, Northern Ireland; 132 dead.

1954, May 26 – United States aircraft carrier *Bennington* jolted by explosions and fire off Quonset Point, R.I.; toll 103 dead, 117 injured.

1954, Sept. 26 – Japanese ferry *Toya Maru* sinks in Tsugaru Strait; 1,172 drowned.

1956, July 26 – Italian liner *Andrea Doria* sinks off Massachusetts coast after collision (July 25) with Swedish motor ship *Stockholm;* 50 killed or missing; 1,652 rescued.

1958, March 1 – Ferryboat breaks up near Istanbul, Turkey, in Sea of Marmara; at least 238 die.

1960, March 4 – French munition ship blows up in harbor of Havana, Cuba, killing 75–100 and injuring 200.

1961, April 8 – 212 persons lost as British liner *Dara* burns in Persian Gulf.

1961, July 8 – Portuguese ship *Save* runs aground off Mozambique and explodes, killing 259.

1961, Sept. 3 – Excursion ship *Vencedor* sinks near Buenaventura, Colombia; 150 reported lost.

1963, April 10 – United States nuclear submarine *Thresher*, with 129 aboard, is lost in North Atlantic.

1963, May 4 – Motor launch sinks in Upper Nile, at Maghagha, Egypt; 206 Muslim pilgrims drown.

1964, Feb. 11 – Destroyer *Voyager* collides with aircraft carrier *Melbourne* off Ulladulla, Australia, and sinks with loss of 85 seamen.

1965, May 23 – 150 believed lost as ferry capsizes in Shire River in Malawi.

1967, July 29 – Fire and explosions aboard U. S. aircraft carrier *Forrestal* kill 134 men on duty off coast of Vietnam.

Bibliography

Blair, Clay, Jr., *Diving for Pleasure and Treasure*. Cleveland and New York, World Publishing Company, 1960.

De Borhegyi, Suzanne, *Ships, Shoals and Amphoras*. New York, Holt, Rinehart & Winston, 1961.

DeFoe, Daniel, *Robinson Crusoe*. New York, The Heritage Press, 1930.

De la Croix, Robert, *Mysteries of the Sea*. New York, The John Day Company, 1957.

Eckert, Allen W., "The Mystery of the Lost Patrol." *American Legion Magazine*, April, 1962.

Franzén, Anders, "Ghost from the Depths: The Warship Vasa." *National Geo-*

graphic Magazine, January, 1964.

Frost, Honor, *Under the Mediterranean.* London, Routledge and Kegan Paul Ltd., 1963.

Gaddis, Vincent, *Invisible Horizons.* Philadelphia and New York, Chilton Books, 1965.

Goldsmith-Carter, George, *Sailors Sailors.* London, Paul Hamlyn Ltd., 1966.

Karraker, Cyrus H., *The Hispaniola Treasure.* University of Pennsylvania Press, 1934.

Keach, Lt. Comdr. Donald L., "Down to the Thresher by Bathyscaph." *National Geographic Magazine,* June, 1964.

Keeble, Peter, *Ordeal by Water.* New York, Doubleday & Company, 1958.

Link, Marion Clayton, "Exploring the Drowned City of Port Royal." *National Geographic Magazine,* February, 1960.

Link, Marion Clayton, *Sea Diver.* New York, Holt, Rinehart & Winston, 1961.

Lonsdale, Adrian L. and Kaplan, H. R., *A Guide to Sunken Ships in American Waters.* Arlington, Virginia, Compass Publications, Inc., 1964.

Martin, O. L., Jr., *The Titanic—50 Years Later.* Science and the Sea, U.S. Naval Oceanographic Office, Washington, D.C., 1967.

Marx, Robert F., "Columbus's Last Two Ships Found in Jamaica." *Argosy,* September, 1968.

Marx, Robert F., "My Month As Robinson Crusoe." *Argosy,* November, 1968.

Marx, Robert F., "Port Royal." *Oceans,* June, 1969.

May, Ernest R., and the Editors of Life, *The Progressive Era,* Vol. 9, 1901–1917. New York, Time Inc., 1964.

Neider, Charles, *Great Shipwrecks and Castaways.* New York, Harper and Brothers, 1952.

Peterson, Mendel, *History Under the Sea.* Smithsonian Pub. 4538, 1965.

Piccard, Jacques, "Piccard Drifts with Gulf Stream." *The New York Times,* August 20, 1969.

Riesberg, Lt. Harry E. and Mikalow, A. A., *Fell's Guide to Sunken Treasure Ships of the World.* New York, Fredrick Fell, Inc., 1965.

Sanderson, Ivan T., "The Spreading Mystery of the Bermuda Triangle." *Argosy,* August, 1968.

Stick, David, *Graveyard of the Atlantic.* The University of North Carolina Press, 1952.

Stowe, Leland, "The Real Robinson Crusoe." *Reader's Digest,* November, 1968.

Taylor, James, *Gold From the Sea; the Epic Story of the Niagara's Bullion.* Sydney, The Australasian Publishing Co. Pty. Ltd., 1942.

Throckmorton, Peter, "Thirty-three Centuries Under the Sea." *National Geographic Magazine,* May, 1960.

Wagner, Kip, "Drowned Galleons Yield Spanish Gold." *National Geographic Magazine,* January, 1965.

Wagner, Kip and Taylor, L. B., *Pieces of Eight.* New York, E. P. Dutton & Co., 1967.

Wilkins, Harold T., *Strange Mysteries of Time and Space.* New York, The Citadel Press, 1959.

Printed in Great Britain
by Amazon.co.uk, Ltd.,
Marston Gate.